BRUEGEL

THE DRAWINGS

COMPLETE EDITION

BY LUDWIG MÜNZ

PHAIDON

© 1961 PHAIDON PRESS LTD., 5 CROMWELL PLACE, LONDON S.W.7
FIRST PUBLISHED 1961
SECOND IMPRESSION 1968

PHAIDON PUBLISHERS INC., NEW YORK
DISTRIBUTORS IN THE UNITED STATES: FREDERICK A. PRAEGER INC.
111 FOURTH AVENUE, NEW YORK, N.Y. 10003
LIBRARY OF CONGRESS CATALOG CARD NUMBER: 68–18907

Translated from
the German manuscript
by Luke Herrmann

SBN 7148 1237 4

MADE IN GREAT BRITAIN
PRINTED BY HUNT BARNARD AND CO. LTD., AYLESBURY

FOREWORD

THIS is a posthumous publication. It is the last major work that Ludwig Münz left ready for the press. His startlingly sudden death on the afternoon of March 7, 1957, while he was leading a discussion group at the Rembrandt Congress in Munich, brought to an end both his scholarly activity, hitherto undiminished despite long illness, and also the rich work of a lifetime, which was thorough and many-sided.

Münz was born in Vienna on January 6, 1889, and always felt himself attached to that city. In the years of his training as an art historian, Hamburg, where he spent several years, as well as Vienna, was of importance for him. In Vienna it was the personality of Max Dvořák, in Hamburg the Warburg Institute, which were decisive influences at the start of his academic career.

In the world of scholarship Münz is best known as an authority on Rembrandt. *Federzeichnungen von Rembrandt und Bol* was the title of his first article, published in 1924, and his last, posthumous article deals with *Rembrandts Vorstellung vom Antlitz Christi*. The most extensive of his works on Rembrandt is the two-volume critical edition of Rembrandt's etchings, published by the Phaidon Press in 1952.

The best evidence of his knowledge of Dutch painting of the time of Rembrandt is his annotated edition of Alois Riegl's *Holländisches Gruppenporträt* (1931). The book *Die Kunst Rembrandts und Goethes Sehen*, published shortly after this, in 1934, contains the first results of Münz's interest in Goethe as an artist. Fifteen years later, in *Goethes Zeichnungen und Radierungen* (1949), he devoted a broader examination to this phenomenon of the amateur activity of a universal mind. This book remains the fullest on Goethe as a draughtsman. Here Münz was interested in discovering the essential qualities of the creative element in the field of the visual arts, and these were also the actual theme of an investigation even more explicitly devoted to the bases of creative artistic activity, namely, his book *Die plastischen Arbeiten Blinder*, published in 1934.

Contemporary art and literature naturally took their place among the interests of the art historian Münz. Thus he was on terms of friendship with three of the leading personalities of the artistic life of Vienna in the fruitful first decades of this century; namely Karl Kraus, Oskar Kokoschka, and Adolf Loos. He also wrote about the last two of these. One of his final publications is a small book about Loos published in Milan in 1956; and he was the executor of the literary and artistic estate of this great architect.

Finally the Catalogues of the Exhibitions which he arranged in the Vienna Akademie der Bildenden Künste (*Oesterreichische Landschaftsmalerei des 19. Jahrhunderts*, 1954; *Oesterreichische Landschaftsmalerei von Schindler bis Klimt*, 1955) bear lasting witness to Münz's knowledge of the art of the nineteenth century. At the same time these exhibitions are evidence of another of Münz's fields of activity, that is his museum work. The tasks and problems of the exhibition and presentation of works of art in a museum had always been matters about which he thought, and which he put into practice for the first time many years ago, in 1933, when, in collaboration with Ernst Garger, he rearranged the display of the Greek vases in the Oesterreichisches Museum für angewandte Kunst. Wider opportunities in this capacity were given to him, when, early in 1947, after having spent nine years as a refugee in London, he was re-called to his native city as Director of the Picture Gallery of the Akademie der bildenden Künste. In the years after his return he carried out the re-hanging of this valuable, though not very large, collection of paintings. In tackling this work the question of the restoration of the paintings played an important part. Münz had already long concerned himself with the delicate problems of restoration, particularly during his years in London. To each of these tasks Münz gave himself with the great devotion and intensity which were natural to him in all his work. These qualities are noticeable in the arrangement of the galleries themselves, – here Münz sought an unpretentious and as far as possible impersonal objectivity, – and to an even greater extent in the academic forcefulness with which he controlled the collection and commented on it in new catalogues (published 1949–1955). In his lectures to the students of the Vienna Akademie, which he gave in his capacity as Director of the Gallery, he resumed in the last years of his life an activity for which he had already much earlier shown a particular gift when he lectured at the Viennese Volkshochschulen.

This pedagogic bent was a characteristic which was of equal importance for Münz both as a man and as a scholar. In the listing above of some of his scholarly publications we have only the outward evidence of his many-sidedness. There can be no doubt that Münz was a learned man; he was also a 'connoisseur'. But he had no declared philosophy of scholarship. Because he realized the danger of scholarship for its own sake, which can so easily lead to arrogance, he rejected for himself the adoption of a distinct academic doctrine. For him the practical usefulness of scholarship was a matter that could be taken for granted. What such an approach to art lacked in a definite system was more than outweighed by an ever lively approach to the individual work of art. In this he always essentially maintained his enthusiasm, and, with great objectivity, preserved something of the sparkle of the first experience. It was in this approach to the work of art, in his reliable eye and his feeling for essential quality, that Münz possessed the best and most important gifts that an art historian can have, and which he must always strive to maintain.

Vienna, 1961   FRITZ NOVOTNY

NOTE

The publishers are responsible for the lay-out of the plates and for the arrangement of the illustrations which follow the introductory text. The versos of two drawings (Cat. Nos. 78 and 87), being rather slight, have been reproduced in the Catalogue, where they will be best understood.

All references to articles published after 1957 have been added by the translator.

Since the death of the author a small number of Bruegel drawings has come to light, and most of these have been published in several articles. An illustrated list of these published re-discovered drawings follows the Catalogue. This has been compiled by the translator, who has abstained from discussion of them, as he did not wish to add anything to Münz's text.

Münz wrote in German; the translation into English is by Mr. Luke Herrmann, Oxford.

London, 1961   PHAIDON PRESS

CONTENTS

INTRODUCTION

THE re-discovery of Bruegel as a draughtsman dates from the early years of the twentieth century. The interest in Bruegel's drawings did not arise much later than that in his paintings. The starting point for modern Bruegel studies is the book published in 1905–1907 by Hulin de Loo and Bastelaer. This also includes the first catalogue of the drawings. Karl Tolnay follows in 1925 with his *Die Zeichnungen Pieter Bruegels*, in which all those drawings which he considered genuine are reproduced. Since then interest in Bruegel's paintings and in his drawings has grown even further. A series of long lost drawings has been re-discovered, and it is more than ever the concern of art historians, making full use of the discoveries and mistakes of the earlier pioneering studies, to re-create a true picture of Bruegel's art. In the present book this leads to an approach which is in some ways different to the methods used by several of the earlier scholars. It seemed a more important task to learn by the detailed study of each individual line through the continual re-examination of the original drawings, than to waste too much time on theories, such as that of the 'macchia' of Bruegel, or that concerned with his 'all-embracing genius'. In the end only the continually repeated examination and comparison of the works of art themselves can lead us to the beginnings of an understanding of them. But, of course, this does not mean that the conclusions of the intellectual and human approach in such researches can be neglected. Only the excesses of expressionist art historical writing should be avoided. In the second edition of his book on Pieter Bruegel's drawings Tolnay himself, without materially altering his text, recognized a number of further drawings as originals by Bruegel. But the present survey also differs from that classification. The number of original drawings by Bruegel known today totals some one hundred and fifty-six, while Tolnay reproduced one hundred and twenty-three drawings. The small number of the surviving drawings is partially accounted for by the fact that Bruegel, as we read in Carel van Mander, himself destroyed a large part of his satirical sheets in order to spare his wife any unpleasantness. What is left divides itself into three groups: some fifty landscapes, seventy-seven *naer het leven* studies, and the remainder – twenty-eight sheets – are drawings of large compositions, which are mostly the surviving drawings for engravings. It was part of Bruegel's way of life that he wished to influence and teach through his works.

The landscapes have rightly been placed at the head of all classifications of Bruegel's drawings, as this group includes the earliest dated examples. There are drawings from 1552 onwards. The corpus of the drawings thus begins at the time, in 1551, when Bruegel, aged about twenty-four, had become a Master and travelled to Italy, whence he returned to the North and his homeland in the course of the year 1553. Dated landscape drawings are preserved covering the years until almost the end of his life, so that the study of these as a complete group can provide the basis for an assessment of Bruegel's development as a draughtsman throughout the whole of his life.

Next comes the section devoted to the discussion of the *naer het leven* studies, the figure drawings which are all undated, and which Tolnay, although Bruegel used material from these studies for his compositions, published in his book as the last group of drawings. The discussion of these drawings leads on to a short analysis of the surviving picture compositions, in which Bruegel as man and artist sought to influence his contemporaries by his teaching, and his warnings and entreaties.

It stands to reason that during the course of so many years of study devoted to the works of Pieter Bruegel I have been much concerned with the current literature. Outstanding among these publications are Michel's books and articles, and Otto Benesch's especially important review of the second edition of Tolnay's book, *The Drawings of Pieter Bruegel the Elder*.

My thanks are due to all the institutions and private collectors who have helped me in my work, and not least to the publishers themselves, who have also assisted me in my search for new, hitherto unknown, drawings by Bruegel, and who then made it possible for good new photographs to be taken of most of the drawings of Pieter Bruegel.

Vienna, December 1956   LUDWIG MÜNZ

BRUEGEL AS A DRAUGHTSMAN

LANDSCAPES

THE earliest surviving works by Pieter Bruegel are two landscapes of 1552, which were probably already drawn in Italy. By all standards – even when compared with Bruegel's later landscape drawings – they are in their way definitive artistic achievements, with their remarkably uncomplicated and naïve handling. In them, especially in the Paris drawing of a *River Valley*, *with Mountain in Background* (No. 1), a new vision and experience of landscape is revealed. The composite order of the landscape is built up naturally and unhesitatingly. With what appears to be the utmost freedom a piece of nature is portrayed in flickering light. This is achieved by the use of countless larger and smaller dots and lines for the distance, which combine with the almost too effective, rather broader, strokes of the foreground to create the unity of the picture as a whole.

General Formative Influences

DESPITE the individual and novel style of this landscape art, its antecedents, particularly in the North at the time around 1550, must be briefly examined. In the sixteenth century the painting of landscape developed an individual style even earlier than that of genre. Pleasure in one's environment and in nature is a typical product of Renaissance humanism, with its scientific efforts better to understand these. Just as in the 'twenties the *Weltbildlandschaft* with its still schematic structure began with Patinier, so in about 1550 a new development started. For it was then that there began the epoch of the large geographical manuals with panorama-like views, which were reproduced as woodcuts, or later as engravings. Here Münzer's *Kosmographie* precedes Bruegel. Those artists who later continued to work in a similar vein, either individually or in association with Bruegel's friend, the great geographer Ortelius, are thus all more or less connected with Bruegel. An important early example of these extended panorama-like views of cities is that of Antwerp, where Bruegel had become Master in 1551, which was already produced by C. Massys in 1522. Though Bruegel uses the same form as these sheets, in principle he has other objectives. He is not really interested in geographical factors, but is fascinated rather by the actual landscape, with its stillness and its own life independent of man.

As a means of conveying atmosphere, landscape had already been regarded with particular favour long before Bruegel, especially in Germany. Already in 1520, in addition to drawings and paintings, independent representations of landscape are to be found in etchings, at that time the most modern method of reproduction. Among these are Altdorfer's mountainous 'universal landscapes' ('*Weltlandschaften*') and also, as well as the work of the draughtsman Wolf Huber, the succession of later German landscape etchers, such as Virgil Solis, Hirschvogel, and Lautensack, who were older contemporaries of Bruegel, and in some ways had similar ambitions. Like Bruegel, but some time before him, they tried to capture the atmosphere and life of the landscape. However, Bruegel's method of portraying landscape does differ greatly from theirs, especially where, like the German artists, he achieves a feeling of grandeur and immensity, particularly in his mountains. His landscapes never have the elementary heaviness of the nearly contemporary German mountain scenes of Wolf Huber, nor the sentimental warmth and effect of the Venetian landscapes, with which he must have been familiar through the woodcuts after Campagnola. The obvious and almost sentimental feeling of the German artists for mountains and landscape, engendered by daily contact with them, is foreign to Bruegel. Of course the earlier and contemporary achievements of Italian landscape art – the natural feeling of Leonardo da Vinci and then the powerful pathos of the Venetian landscape painters such as Titian and Campagnola – are again and again reflected in the works of these northern artists, and especially in those of Pieter Bruegel.

Closer Influences on Bruegel's Development as a Landscape Artist, especially in his own country

Having mentioned these general influences, which can be applied to the whole of this period, we must now turn to those artists from whose works Bruegel, in his youth, and already in his homeland, learnt more specifically for the apparently objective and quiet, yet living, landscapes. There are a number of northern, more especially Netherlandish, artists, in whose work Bruegel found models for his intimate close-ups as well as for the wide spaces of his large and extensive instructive and interpretative compositions (*Lern- und Lesebilder*) of nature in his own country. Bruegel was an artist who, because he could think to a conclusion what the others had aimed at, could thus create such free landscapes.

Hieronymus Bosch, under whose influence Bruegel always worked from the very beginning in his satirical compositions (even in the first of these sheets of 1556), is also, in a deeper sense, the actual creator of his way of drawing landscape. In the paintings and drawings of Bosch there is already to be found – as is also found much later in the work of Bruegel – the vision of a luminous piece of nature (fig. 1*), in the portrayal of which both artists used a masterly, unexpectedly temperamental, and dynamically candid series of single strokes, especially in the foreground. The drawings of Bruegel – the humanistically educated man who worked some thirty years after the death of Bosch – do, however, differ in one detail from those of the artist who is his most closely related forerunner: that is in the objectivity of their line, drawn as it were for eternity, in which, dissolved in dots and strokes, and yet clearly arranged in space, a world is re-created. In this Bruegel's spacious drawings have their own type of vitality, though, in the thoroughness with which, from the very start, the details are formed, just as in geographical illustrations, they may seem like works designed for reproduction. Everything which points to a rapid sketch is purposely omitted, and the slightly stronger strokes of the very close foreground fully combine with the more precise build-up of the distant landscape in achieving the illusion.

The most closely related forerunner of this illusion-creating line is Dürer, perhaps especially in the landscape background of his extensive etching of 1518, *Die Kanone* (fig. 2); though with the same artistic materials Bruegel's portrayal of nature is much more alive. It is a feature of Bruegel, who

*Fig. 1 and the following text illustrations will be found after p. 36.

in his work always combines the most advanced methods with those which are passed down by tradition, that in his landscape drawings, which fashion the light and shade of the scene with great liveliness, he never uses broad and strong washes, as is sometimes the case in Italian landscape drawings. It was, in fact, Bruegel's achievement, that, advancing slowly beyond the accepted graphic methods for individual details, he knew how to create a whole world, in which, as never before, sky, rocks, mountains and ravines stand before us in convincing reality. Whether or not Dürer's style was consciously or unconsciously a decisive stimulus, in his youth Bruegel could learn everything else which related to the portrayal of landscape from the older artists of his own country, in order to develop and transform it. Already since Patinier it had been the aim of Netherlandish landscape art to portray landscape in its true form, avoiding its division into disconnected planes, and Bruegel's actual teacher, Pieter Coeck, also already shows in his woodcuts the search for a forcefully unified space, often relying on Italian models.

What Bruegel, however, is seeking, and it is this which leads him to a new and unique landscape art, is a way of achieving an absolutely convincing representation of a piece of nature. It is his aim to capture the illusion of the depth and width of space with a successful and natural arrangement of foreground, middle distance and background, so that these parts are so naturally bound together that the means of their unity also creates an illusion of the continuous breadth and clarity of the space. Though in Bruegel's landscapes the spacious distance often seems to be organically divided from the more colourful and darker tones of the diagonal foreground area, it is so bound up with these in light and darkness that a united and freely moving scene emerges.

The forerunners of such work in the North are the innovators of Italian landscape art, Leonardo and the Venetians. Already before Pieter Bruegel the Netherlanders were fascinated by this. In his earliest youth Bruegel could thus learn the incomplete perception and adaptation of such influences (without having to be aware of the actual sources of these landscape styles) in the works of his teacher Pieter Coeck. Bruegel had also already received the real inspiration for the parallel form of his foregrounds in the works of landscape and genre painters such as his teacher's brother-in-law, Jan van Amstel, the so-called Brunswick Monogrammist, or Cornelis Massys. Throughout his life Bruegel remained loyal to these native conventions. However if one considers the structural composition of the large landscapes, with their diagonal divisions leading into the distance, it must be said that among the older northern artists, whose works Pieter Bruegel could have known at an early date, an arch-mannerist like Martin van Heemskerk had already discovered the most advanced adaptation of the Italian antecedents. At any rate the style of the landscape sketches of Heemskerk stands closer to Bruegel than that of Matthys Cock, who always counts as the chief inspirer of Bruegel's art, though this claim may be true objectively for the 'universal landscape' as a class. In their adaptation of the Italian structure of landscape the drawings of Matthys Cock tend to be more petty and conservative than those of Heemskerk. In Matthys Cock's surviving drawings, and in the etchings after his works by his brother Hieronymus Cock, there is never really that genuine spacious unity which is already to be found in Martin van Heemskerk's sketch books of the middle thirties. In these, in addition to the breaking up of the contours of the landscape into small, outstandingly luminous, individual parts, there are also to be found those large, spirited curved lines which unite the foreground with the more distant landscape. Heemskerk was the first northerner to develop an individual adaptation and transformation of the art of Campagnola. (See figs. 3-5.)

Bruegel's Own Style in connection with Italian Art

FOLLOWING the same principles in his portrayal of landscape, Bruegel, however, already in his earliest drawings, achieved something more unique, new and more fertile. He not only breaks up more completely the contours of the background of the distant landscape, but he also achieves that impressive illusion of a unified and homogeneous landscape vision by his method of stressing the extreme foreground with accentuated and dynamic single lines, as in the river landscape of 1552 (No. 1). It is a vision of nature which only finds still further fulfilment in the seventeenth century with Rembrandt, when the line becomes entirely free with its full impetuosity. Later still the method which Bruegel discovered of depicting landscape by lines without wash – this factor must also be borne in mind – is to be found once again in the wide and spacious landscape vision of Van Gogh, built up by means of single broad strokes of the reed pen.

Bruegel's naïve discovery of an embracing vision of nature in these early drawings is afterwards always to be found in his work. His line becomes ever richer and more varied. But his portrayal of landscape does not always retain the same force of naïve and manifest achievement as in these earliest landscapes, in which the construction has succeeded so convincingly that we are inclined to forget that in them we have a new and fertile method of landscape composition. However, if one bears in mind that in fact an early study of nature, such as the river landscape of 1552 (No. 1), has been carefully thought out and composed, then the attempt to divide Bruegel's drawings into two categories, studies from nature, and compositions, does not seem very profitable. Outstanding examples of Bruegel's freest style of drawing – in discussing these landscape drawings preference must be given to their inner coherence rather than to the purely chronological arrangement – are, then, drawings such as the *View of Waltersspurg* done on the homeward journey of 1553/54 (No. 19) or *The large Rhine landscape* (No. 21) with its extensive sky, in which the illusion of space is delicately and vividly achieved, and earth and broad sky are successfully joined together, seemingly without space-creating coulisses but only by means of darker and lighter strokes. In such drawings Bruegel also becomes the true forerunner of the landscape vision of a Ruisdael or a Koninck. These are works in which man has found the means for a new and deeper realization of the essence of nature, for they convincingly combine in a picture the width and height of the skies and the smallness of the earth.

If, however, one examines Pieter Bruegel's drawings of 1553, the second and last year of his stay in Italy and the year of his departure for his homeland, and keeps as far as possible to the chronological sequence of their production, one can establish, in addition to the extensive panorama-like studies, mostly of distant mountain ranges, which follow the drawings of 1552 in their construction, a group of more openly composed landscapes, which are very close to nature. In these Bruegel draws on the most effective results of what he saw and learnt in Italy. His ability to create a landscape picture by means of dots and small strokes developed very quickly, and already gained further forcefulness in the course of 1553. If at first these drawings give the impression that they owe their colourful and almost concealed dynamic intensity to only one colour – light bistre or darker brown – this is an illusion. The true life and colour of these drawings, with the minute divisions of the system of strokes, is based on the fact that Bruegel accentuates darkness and lightness, and with them the whole illumination, by always using related darker and lighter brown strokes. Thus just by means of this system of delicate strokes in various tones, which seems objectively to render the whole, the individual parts of the landscape achieve their own, unmistakable meaning. Hardly ever

(14)

has another draughtsman had the power of Bruegel to capture every most fleeting and easily over-looked movement in the atmosphere of a landscape, by means of the size, direction and variation of his strokes, and thereby clearly and calmly to render the structure of each individual part. A system of dots gives the most fugitive elements, such as the shadows of clouds over mountain slopes, while the rocks with their accentuated verticals or horizontals are differentiated from the rhythm of the flowing lines of other parts of the landscape. The detail of the landscape naturally grows richer and more accomplished. Not always quite so successful is Bruegel's construction of the landscape which in its breath and with its high horizon continually becomes more and more of an instructive and interpretative picture of nature, and where he has to assimilate in his 'universal landscapes' the stimulus of his homeland – of a Patinier. The full development of such Bruegel landscapes and the extensive changes in their style depend on the continually renewed analysis of the art of Campagnola. In the latter's work Bruegel finds the same method of a strongly accentu-ated foreground fully in sympathy with the broad distance of the mountain ranges. But it is even more significant that from 1553 onwards the use of the human figure, with its movement, is to be found as an essential part of the whole landscape in Bruegel's work. This also originates from Campagnola. In the drawing of 1553, *Landscape with River and Mountains* (No. 4), the figures, some of whom point into the distance, while others are resting, or, with rapid movements, are going from the foreground into the landscape, are new and decisive developments taken from Italian examples. A precedent for this can already be found in Campagnola's woodcuts of about thirty years earlier.

Because we believe that Bruegel's large instructive and interpretative pictures of landscape, particularly the engravings of the large landscape series, are something unique, we must consider what it is that differentiates Bruegel, who was certainly inwardly an emotional observer, though wishing to remain objectively cool in his art, from one of the fathers of modern Italian landscape painting and drawing – from Leonardo da Vinci. When Leonardo draws mountains, or creates the most marvellous drawings of natural disaster and its upheavals, this is based on the knowledge of, and research into, the actual causes of such happenings. In contrast to such research work – to such concern with the creation and destruction of the natural – Bruegel is rather a quiet observer of what he sees and of what he must take into consideration as a part of nature. Thus he only feels obliged to report, so to speak, objectively, seriously and categorically about the life and suffering of nature, without having to give any account of the causes of such manifestations of nature. The remarkable and characteristic feature of Bruegel's way of seeing is, that, with the exception of the two first drawings, he was hardly fascinated by the beauty of the landscape in Italy itself. [I am convinced that the view of Rome (No. A24), which has hitherto always been listed as a work by Bruegel of this period, is not by Bruegel himself, and that the drawing of Fondi (No. A6), which of late has also been mentioned in the books, is certainly not the work of Bruegel.] What next moves him is the way in which sky and earth are joined together – as in the *Landscape with Walled Town* (No. 3) – and the changeability of the appearance of nature in varying lights, though in most of his drawings Bruegel seeks to depict the scene in bright light. Already on his return journey in 1553, however, Bruegel begins to be fascinated by high mountains, rugged rocks, steep passes and the view into broad and low-lying valleys. These things so gripped him that for a whole period of his activity they became almost an exclusive subject for him. Thus the large landscape compositions of moun-tains and lonely wooded lakes, which all look so natural, are reproduced in this book in association with the studies of mountain ranges and rocks, despite the fact that some of them were certainly only drawn in 1555 or 1556. What Carel van Mander wrote in a much quoted passage, that Bruegel

(15)

devoured the Alps in order to spit them out again in his homeland, is true in a deeper sense. From then onwards, when he paints or draws his 'universal landscapes', Bruegel is always interested in mountains and in remarkable and picturesque rock formations. Here, however, it ought to be remembered that the love of picturesque rock details and of the distant view towards high mountains is, already from the time of Van Eyck, essentially part of the Netherlandish artists' conception of the landscape of their homeland. In the Louvre *Virgin and Child with the Chancellor Rolin* there are a view of Liége, the landscape of the Maas valley with its picturesque rocks and a mountainous landscape in the far distance.

In his large mountain landscapes Bruegel has completely transformed for his own purposes the diagonal picture composition of Campagnola. The *Mountain Landscape* of 1553 (No. 4) is the leading example of this. That these large, seemingly so natural, mountain landscapes have in reality been carefully composed can largely be proved by the fact that in them parts of the single landscape studies of 1553 are repeated in the details of the foregound and distance. The most important surviving documents of this landscape art of Bruegel, which were executed in the late fifties and probably also even after 1560, are the large landscape etchings published by Hieronymus Cock. It should be mentioned that Bruegel in his grasp of a landscape, of its spacious atmosphere, its inner life and of the figures that stress its character, recreated its essential mood. It is a vision of landscape which is above all of vital importance for the art of the southern Netherlands – one need only think of the landscapes of Rubens. Bruegel is also the first – and this ought to be stressed – to give his landscape etchings titles that are pregnant with atmosphere: thus, for example, *Plaustrum belgicum* is the title of one in which he wishes to give a picture of his homeland, and in another the title *Euntes in Emaus* gives the three figures of the pilgrims clear and moving meaning and purpose in such a legendary landscape in their search for a home. If one wishes to seek further explanations in the world known through his *near het leven* drawings and compositions, for Bruegel's predilection when composing his landscapes for cliffs and derelict boulders, one could state with truth that Bruegel always retains those elements of a landscape which are permanent, which remain when storm and weather are played out. Picturesque as they are in their individual forms they fascinate him, just as later in his *naer het leven* studies and compositions it is not the brilliant and outstanding individual that plays a leading rôle, but rather the basic element of society – ordinary men with their typical appearance and their picturesque movements.

Of the large instructive and interpretative pictures (*Lern- und Lesebilder*) of nature two are dateable: the badly preserved study for the alpine landscape of 1555 (No. 13) and also a drawing at Chatsworth, which I and other students have dated to 1556 (No. 16). Judging by its shape, this second drawing must have been the model for a series of smaller landscape engravings, which was not, however, carried out. The fact that the *verso* is covered with red chalk also points to this. A number of the completed landscape studies of 1553 also had the same smaller format. Thus it seems possible that a smaller series was planned. In addition to these complete and uniformly finished drawings of the fifties there is also another group of landscape drawings of this period. These are large, quickly executed and, fundamentally incomplete compositions. They form an individual type in Bruegel's landscape art. The first example of these is the *St. Jerome* of 1553 (No. 22). Then there follows a tree and landscape drawing dated 1554 (No. 23), concerning the authenticity of which there is some doubt, but which, together with the *verso* of this sheet, provides such important information about Bruegel's methods – his enlivening of the middle distance by means of trees through which the distance can be seen, and his use of figures – that they are here reproduced in the context of the original drawings. For this reason the study on the *verso*, with the two horsemen riding towards each other, is also reproduced (No. 24). The last sheet of this group is the composition with the *Rest on the Flight* (No. 25), which, of course, does not belong to the early period, but, with its deliberate colourful accentuation of parts of the landscape, cannot have been drawn until 1559. The surviving study of Reggio for the *Battle of Messina* (No. 26), which has been much worked over, must also date from this time. The confidence of the line speaks for the late completion of this drawing, but the inspiration for it may have been notes dating from 1552, as during his stay in Italy Bruegel visited Sicily.

The year 1559 brings a turning point in Bruegel's work as a landscape draughtsman. For several years, 1559–1562/64, he produced smaller landscapes, looser in line and almost sentimental in character. Judging by the style of their line, none of these can have been meant for reproduction. These must be discussed separately. At the same time the large landscapes, designed for reproduction, continued, for, as has been said, the series of these cannot already have been completed before 1560.

Small Landscapes

NEXT we must discuss the antecedents of the so-called Small Landscapes of Pieter Bruegel. If Bruegel owes his vision of the 'universal landscape' to Matthys Cock and his brother Hieronymus Cock, who had already become his publisher in 1556 and who had probably earlier arranged his journey to Rome, then this influence is even more valid for the whole group of landscapes, above all those of the years 1559 to 1561, in which Bruegel depicted on a small scale scenes of his immediate surroundings, Flemish villages, hamlets and castles, in addition to imaginary rock landscapes and valleys. In 1559 the firm of Hieronymus Cock had published a series of such small, intimate close-up views of village landscapes. These are all genuine continuations and developments of the close-up scenes of the generation before Bruegel. The words *naer het leven* on the title page exactly denote their characteristics; love of the homeland and the intimate representation of its most typical scenes, humble though they may be. They must have had a great success, for in 1561 a second series appeared, which was also reprinted several times. These landscape engravings have such inward animation that they have long been considered as works by Bruegel himself. Even in the seventeenth century further states were issued, which were attributed to Bruegel by the Amsterdam publisher Vischer.

We know today that these small landscape engravings did not originate from Bruegel himself. In the first instance Burchard named Hans Bol, a slightly younger artist whom Bruegel must certainly have known, as the author of these engravings, for at a later date, after Bruegel's death, Bol executed *Autumn* and *Winter*, which were very similar in style, in the series of the Seasons, of which Bruegel had only completed *Spring* and *Summer*, for the publisher Cock. If this were true then Bol would in effect have been the creator of this new, intimate vision of landscape. The attribution of this whole series to Hans Bol seems to me to be as unconvincing as the other attribution to Cornelis Cort. Bol or Cort can only be considered as the authors of the four sheets which later completed the series. (See figs. 6–7.) There is, however, much to be said for the argument that the author of most of the drawings for this series is Bruegel's publisher, Hieronymus Cock, himself. In these engravings, and in the drawings for them, there is to be found a highly distinctive method of forming the foliage of the trees by means of small and schematic curves. The same method is also to be seen in the engravings which Hieronymus Cock made after the landscape drawings of his brother Matthys. The summary character of the figures in these is also the same as in the small landscape series. They are figures which sometimes seem to have the meagre character of puppets. There is much in favour of the proposition that these studies from life, which give an intimate close-up view, originated with an older artist than Hans Bol, namely Hieronymus Cock. [Some-times, in the retouching with the burin, especially of the figures, the coarser hand of the engraver, one of the brothers Duotecum, is noticeable, as it is in Hieronymus Cock's engravings of the Roman ruins, of which one series has also been retouched by the same hand.] It is, however, also of decisive importance that the Dutch landscape artists of the seventeenth century, who, in the open and parallel arrangements of their foreground broke away from the Italian example, found far-reaching inspiration in these engravings of Hieronymus Cock. It is also high time to remind ourselves that the outstanding creator of this type of landscape before Bruegel was not Hieronymus Cock himself, but that he must have been that artist whom we call the Master of the Errera Sketchbooks. He can on no account be identified with Matthys Cock, while Benesch's designation of Vereyken as the Master of the Female Half-Lengths has one thing in its favour – that it indicates the genuine environ-ment of such landscape art, namely that following of Patinier to which Herri met de Bles belongs. (See fig. 8.) In this connection it is further important to assert once again that already before the year 1550 Cornelis Massys as well as Jan van Amstel created such close-up pictures.

Bruegel's Small Landscapes

It is clear that Bruegel used the inspiration of the Hieronymus Cock series for his small landscape drawings. On this basis, however, he created something entirely unique – those of his drawings which are the most delicate and most resolved in light and colour. Judging by the surviving examples the new series begins with a landscape drawn in the lightest bistre with rapid and fundamentally unarchitectural strokes. In this (No. 27) one sees a steep path leading to an old castle, and a chapel beneath a huge rock-face, while in the foreground on the right a wide footbridge crosses the valley to the lightest and most barely indicated of landscapes with castles and hills, which is lost or dis-solved in the distance. Further drawings of 1559 and 1560 again repeat this play with fantastic crags and also the melting of the distance, in which steep paths, leading to rock-faces, alternate with broad river beds, as in the drawings in Berlin and Amsterdam (Nos. 29 and 30), while once again the narrowness of such mountain tracks between the towering rocks is dramatically emphasized. In 1561 there follow still further studies of lone castles. Their technique, by which Bruegel aims to capture the atmosphere of the landscape, is so widely different from the rest of Bruegel's work, that Tolnay doubted, for example, Count Seilern's drawing (No. 32),* and excluded from Bruegel's corpus a drawing in Berlin (No. 33) which Friedländer had rightly attributed to him. Already in 1560, how-ever, simultaneously with these imaginary landscapes, concerning which one cannot resist the opinion that in these years of crisis Bruegel found escape in this picturesque dreamworld, there appeared a group of intimate homeland landscapes, which show the Flemish village, as no drawing had done before, in the clearest light and in the whole damp everyday atmosphere. These far surpass the small landscape prints of Cock. The newly discovered landscape with the cathedral in the distance (No. 34) belongs to these, as do the most delicate village views, dissolved in light, in which again the

*In his second edition Tolnay withdrew his doubts.

small figures go about their everyday tasks, particularly emphasizing their meaning. The most important examples are those in the Akademie der bildenden Künste in Vienna (No. 35), and those in Paris and Berlin (Nos. 36 and 37). But the choice of favourite subject again changes, swinging back in 1561 to the views with castles and ruins, and then leading to grandiose commemorative pictures, such as the landscape with the sunrise in Paris (No. 41), in which the rocks rise terribly steeply on the right, or the landscape with the gorge in the Boymans-van Beuningen Museum, Rotterdam (No. 42). Already in this year Bruegel, in the same very free technique, again begins to undergo a change. The size of the drawings once more becomes larger (the drawing in Besançon, No. 43) and from 1562 onwards the drawings (in Munich and Brunswick, Nos. 44 and 45) are almost of the same size as those of Bruegel's Italian period. The sheet with the blind men (No. 46), as well as the three sheets in the same technique which render with a flickering light effect the towers and bastions of a city (Nos. 47–49) – supposed to be Amsterdam – also belong to this period. The early sixties are known to have been years of crisis in Bruegel's life, which end in 1564 with his marriage and his move to Brussels. The drawings of this time, especially those of the first years, are therefore also important records of Bruegel's inner search, of his vacillation and his restlessness. With almost unbelievable delicacy these landscapes achieve a sense of space in the distance. It seems likely that for Bruegel this rendering of nature and of his environment implied an equivalent to the exorcising of evil, the fight with death – conceptions which held him spellbound in these years. If one considers the principal motifs of such landscapes, their *vanitas* factor, the feeling that everything is transitory becomes obvious. Ruins, collapsed rocks, boulders in the landscape, unexpected holes in these, crevices picturesquely revealed among the cliffs; all these seem to have this meaning. Then, still far removed from the Dutch landscapes of the seventeenth century with their wide, navigable rivers, there are in these drawings of Bruegel, particularly in the vicinity of the sea, the most remarkable obstacles, rocky islands and dangerous reefs, a feature related to the strange rocks spread over the landscape first introduced in the large rocky landscape of about 1555 (No. 12). Other elements of these landscapes seem symbolic of the violent, the powerful, the dominant, and of the fear of these and of the desire to overcome them. The castles on crags, the narrow passes, which often appear and by which one has to go, and the steep tracks in the hills – these, like the rivers, are obstacles to make journeying difficult, and are symbols of the troubles of life, and of the desire to overcome all such obstacles. Simultaneously, and in contrast, there is revealed in the landscapes from 1560 to 1562 the idyllic peacefulness of the villages and of the homeland surroundings. This may well be the interpretation of those delicate landscape scenes of the years after 1561, which, as has already been mentioned, look backwards in their style and are closely related to Bruegel's large drawings of the fifties.

The Large Landscape Drawings of the Later Sixties

IT has already been suggested that the series of the large landscape prints could not have been completed before 1560. As external evidence that Bruegel was still working on these at a later date, it may be mentioned that on the study for the large *St. Jerome* engraving is the date 1560, and that on another drawing of this series the signature takes the form which Bruegel only commonly used after 1560, when he no longer signed 'Brueghel' with an 'h', but simply 'Bruegel'. But more important as evidence for me is the continual ripening of that technique which, by means of somewhat more contrasted shades of brown, makes possible the increased strengthening of the small strokes which achieve the effect of space in the landscape. A landscape like that with the storm (No. 50), which has been inexplicably dated to the early period, can only have been drawn in Bruegel's late period, as is generally accepted by students today, with the exception of Tolnay. The masterly and didactic rendering of the storm-swept waves by dots and cross-hatched lines belongs to this late period. The only surviving Bruegel etching of 1566 also shows a related style. In the large drawn and engraved compositions of the fifties and sixties, however much they undergo changes, landscape is always for Bruegel a means for teaching and interpreting, an area of activity with a high horizon. In the last years of his life this art finds its most complete expression, not in any drawings, but in the powerful paintings of *The Months*. In these last years the world he sees and its landscapes become for him ever more only a part of that which he wants to show; man, what he is and what he experiences, becomes increasingly, and then almost exclusively, his subject. Thus Bruegel's latest surviving landscape drawings are actually compositions for pictures, to which areas of landscape belong as part of the environment. The two surviving sheets of the seasons, *Spring* and *Summer* (Nos. 151 and 152) and the large sheet of *The Bee-Keepers* (No. 154) are evidence of this. But in these there is an illusionistic loosening in the rendering of living nature, which shows how much even at that time Bruegel made use of all that pre-occupied him so strongly for a short period in his small landscapes. His visions of landscape are so unique just for this reason, that behind their seeming objectivity, their hesitant adherence to what actually exists, a heart beats for which 'nature' is something deeply important. This nature has its own life, its own laws of durability and change, and men, with all their faults and all their struggles and pettiness, can only live if they remain faithful to, and integrated with, this larger continuity of nature.

Contemporaries and Imitators

It is important to establish that in his time Bruegel was only the *primus inter pares* in his art, as is proved, for instance, by the drawings of Vienne and Lyons by the Master of Stuttgart, the Anonymus Fabriczy. Nor, in addition, is it superfluous to point to the ways in which Bruegel's style of landscape drawing was used by his contemporaries and imitators. Artists such as Hans Bol or Cornelis Cort follow extensively Bruegel's style of the fifties, which lends itself so well to reproduction by engravings. In somewhat later years the reception of Bruegel's work by artists such as Jacques Savery or his brother Roeland is rather different. Their starting point is frequently Bruegel's rendering of landscape, such as in the small landscape drawings of the sixties, with their somewhat erratic and glimmering line. Jacques Savery's style is especially important in this context, and is easy to identify by means of his signed etchings; nevertheless even an expert such as Tolnay, in the 1952 edition of his book, included among the works of Bruegel of 1559 a sheet which with its rounded line is clearly by Jacques Savery. In addition it is extremely important that Bruegel's large landscape drawings were continually copied. A whole series of such copies must originate from Bruegel's sons; as a landscape draughtsman, particularly in connection with his father's drawings, Jan Brueghel the Elder is the most important. A large group of drawings, especially the upright forest pictures related to Muziano, are the work of Jan Brueghel the Elder, and with these it is very difficult to ascertain whether there were also originally drawings of the same themes by the father.

At any rate the drawing inscribed *a rypa* (No. A24), which Egger had attributed to Pieter Bruegel the Elder, and the authenticity of which had actually already been doubted by Gustav Glück, shows, in its schematic style, in the colour of the ground, and in the curved line which unifies whole areas, a far stronger relationship to the technique of Jan Brueghel the Elder than to that of Pieter Bruegel the Elder. The drawing of *Basrode* (Nos. A26 and A27), which exists in numerous versions, also belongs to this type. Thus there is a whole series of drawings, which are included in the catalogue, of which it is not at all clear whether they are copies by one of the sons of the work of the father, or whether they are original and independent landscape compositions. Here there is a wide field still open for research, and it should also be mentioned in closing that as late as 1620 Pieter Brueghel the Younger was still drawing in the same pointilistic style which actually originated in Bruegel's drawings of the sixties.

THE "NAER HET LEVEN" STUDIES

THE second group of Bruegel's drawings is made up of the studies of single and two or more figures. These are generally known as the '*naer het leven*' studies, because these words are inscribed on most of these drawings. It is in keeping with the humanist and stoic leanings of a number of Netherlandish artists of the second third of the sixteenth century, that they are eager to portray everything with everyday reality in their sketches and pictures: *naer het leven*, which means from life. The originator of such inscriptions is van Eyck, who on the Arnolfini double portrait inscribed *Johannes de Eyck fuit hic*' and added '*als ich es sah*'. The pleasure in doing this lay in the ability to create reality in light and shade and colour without keeping to the conventional dramatic poses, such as were used in religious painting. In the sixteenth century, around and after 1550, the term '*naer het leven*' seems to have spread to the southern Netherlands; Bruegel is by no means the first and only artist who inscribed his drawings in this way. In the first instance this inscription is found on landscape drawings, in which the aim was really to re-create a piece of nature. Hendrik van Cleve included it on a drawing of Rome, which dates from the early fifties, and an important series of intimate close-up views of homeland villages, published by Hieronymus Cock in 1559, was described as *naer het leven* on the title page, as has already been mentioned. At this time reality was something fascinating for men, just because of its unevennesses and difficulties, and of its remoteness from officially accepted beauty. This was so not only in landscape. Thus when Bruegel inscribes most of his figure studies with the words '*naer het leven*', and adds to these colour notes for the individual pieces of clothing, he is again, in fact, only following an existing tradition. The inclusion of such colour notes is already to be found in figure sketches of the fifteenth century.

Thus, just as there is a tradition for the inscription of these studies, unique though Bruegel's drawings of this type are, so the same may be said in principle of the choice of the figures in these studies. Practically none of these studies shows people of the higher classes. Basically they all portray people, who in their way represent the average existence of the world, leaving out the possibility of good fortune which enables individuals to rise: peasants, beggars, gipsies, wood-cutters, market women, soldiers and sailors. These are the people who are to be found again and again in Bruegel's drawings. It is as if in his method of working from life he also wanted to note their movements – *naer het leven* –

particularly the unconsciously typical ones which were wholly characteristic. Nor must one forget that since the end of the fifteenth century wayfaring people were continually being represented in drawings and engravings.

The back views, and those figures which in their momentary and yet genuine covering of the face seem to catch for ever the rugged being of the man as one of the crowd, as well as in his 'I am as you find me' individuality, hold a decisive place among these drawings of Bruegel. His method is far removed from the extensive individualisation and underlining of personality which is found in Italian art.

The motives which lead to such drawings are not easy to determine. But one thing is certain – whether it is Bruegel, or later the Japanese Hokusai, who draws human figures in this way and uses them in his compositions – that such figures are created at times of crisis, in which primitive faith undergoes a change; and the representational religious picture with its full-face portrayals, in front of which the viewer can stand devoutly, must also change. At such times there is a new sort of spiritualisation of religious painting, because, apparently devalued for the time being and robbed of its exclusiveness, it is placed right in the centre of life. Man is no longer only a servant who must stand gazing at the religious picture from a respectful distance. Despite his pettiness he takes himself more seriously and believes in a different way in **a reality** and in its consequences, and thus also in the events and facts of the Bible story. The introduction of the back view as a thing worthy of portrayal is one of the most characteristic factors of the contemporary spiritual, and hence visual, changes caused by the clash between faith and humanism. While at earlier times the viewer stood facing the picture, he is now behind the people seen from the back, who are perhaps spectators at a Crucifixion, and is no more than a further, though distant, witness. This also introduces into religious painting the possibility of including a whole series of different thoughts as themes of the composition. For only now is it possible to show simultaneously with the Crucifixion – the sacrificial death of Christ – the varying reactions to this event of groups of people widely differing in character but accurately characterized. At the same time as such changes in religious painting there also re-appears a form of painting which had not been known in European art since classical times – the genre picture with its delight in looking at the everyday events of life. Thus Bruegel, in his portrayal of figures in this way, again has a whole series of forerunners in Northern, particularly Dutch and Flemish, art. Perhaps it is superfluous, in this connection, to draw attention to the part played in such representations by the more intimate work of the miniaturists in the *Livres d'heures*. It is, however, more important to point out that true prototypes are also to be found for this type of figure, this characterization of remarkable and unexpected poses, which show men as if they were secretly observed, not quietly at rest, but in transitory movement.

One of the best examples of this type of representation is probably the drawing of the Crucifixion after van Eyck, which comes from the circle of Bosch and is preserved at the Albertina (fig. 9). Here also there are such back views, people in the crowd, chance spectators in a type of picture in which, with all its strictness and harshness of line, there is already to be found a true illusionist rendering of solid bodies by means of dots and small strokes. There is also in Bruegel's work, as has already been mentioned, a whole series of figures which in their outward appearance – the face is perhaps entirely hidden by a hat – give an impression of being scurrilous. However, with these one should not forget that a good number of such portrayals were meant to do nothing more than to give a glimpse of life which is unconventional and yet typical; achieved, if one likes, with apparently pessimistic humour. Thus when, for instance, P. Kunst before him, and Bruegel himself draws a bagpiper striking up for an ample peasant couple, they show – and this is true even more of Bruegel at a later date – that pose and that movement of the limbs which are wholly characteristic of such bagpipers when they strike up. It is a portrayal which, despite the complete anonymity of the figure, gives the most excellent characterization of his profession and standing. Its roots in Flemish art are probably in those compositions of Bosch, in which he, in a clever *pars pro toto* setting, shows the village musician, as the encourager of lewdness, made up of only two parts, his instrument and his paunch, and yet fully characterized in this way. (See fig. 11.)

One must not close this short discussion of the precursors of the *naer het leven* studies without mention of one further artist, whom Bruegel must have known in his youth, Jan van Amstel, the Brunswick Monogramist, who had already portrayed back views and transitory movements of people with great naturalness and realism.

The Technique of the *Naer Het Leven* Drawings

CONTRARY to the belief of a number of scholars, who wanted primarily to see in these drawings an individual artistic category, the study of their technique gives the following results: the chalk drawing, which was probably done from nature, is visible in practically all these drawings; likewise the original chalk inscriptions on these drawings are bigger and more quickly written than the words strengthened with ink in the finished drawings. Whether originally sketched with black or red chalk, the drawings were then completed in the studio with dark and light brown inks, probably mostly bistre. That the groundwork was originally in chalk is proved above all by the fact that there are pure black or red chalk drawings, especially of animals and of people in movement, on the back of some completed *naer het leven* studies – the inscription *naer het leven* was only added to the completed drawing. In connection with these drawings it is important to notice that in them Bruegel was so intent to catch the fleeting movement that often, particularly with the animals, he drew the head or the legs in several different positions in relation to the one body. Then, when completing the drawing, the final choice is made, and that position which Bruegel considered the most characteristic is chosen.

Because this fundamental process of drawing has been overlooked until now, scholars such as Tolnay have been able to accept only the fully completed sheets as the work of Bruegel, while other drawings – for instance the sheet with the shepherd (No. 62), which has not been entirely worked over and in which one sees the pointing hands in various positions – have simply been dismissed, without any reason, as not being by Bruegel. There is in fact one further particular criterion in judging the authenticity of Bruegel's drawings, which is also not unimportant in dating them: the handwriting of the inscribed colour notes, which are found to right and left of the figures which he outlined in ink. The style of Bruegel's writing changes in the course of his life from an at first somewhat wild to a continually more careful form. His writing also varies in size – at the later period it is mostly small. Thus there is little sense in rejecting drawings on which the character of the inscription is fully in accord with that on undoubted drawings by Bruegel, because they are apparently unfinished, or because the style does not seem to reach the standards of the best studies, or because the chalk outline has been largely rubbed away.

However, there is of course also an organic development in the technique of Bruegel's draughtsmanship, though this can only slowly become apparent with a more intimate grasp of his work.

The changes in the way of inking in the studies in the studio as well as the changes in the style of the handwriting lead to the recognition of changes in the style of the draughtsmanship, which are of importance for the dating of the drawings. The prevailing assumption that Bruegel's *naer het leven* drawings only begin in 1559 is disproved by the fact that, for example, a stag is to be found on drawing No. 52 which was already to be seen in a similar position on the drawing with St. Jerome as a Hermit of 1553 (No. 22). The next criterion for the dating of the *naer het leven* studies is provided by the completed composition drawings of 1556. On the sheet, for example, with the big fish eating the little fish (No. 128) full use is already made quite spontaneously of that method of combining hatchings drawn in different directions to achieve the illusion of the modelling of the body of the large fish, by means of which the direction of the curves of the body is emphasized, together with the colourful breaking up of the whole by means of small curves and rings. The roots of this type of modelling are clearly and expressively seen – to name only examples that are close in date – above all in the drawings of Dürer and his followers, and perhaps in a wilder and more expressive form in Schäufelein. A change in this style of draughtsmanship is to be found in the drawings of older contemporaries of Bruegel. Here the modelling is emphasized by the illusionistic use of dark and light shading, in which the expressive character of the lines must naturally be made to harmonize. Mannerist artists of the Netherlands, above all Martin van Heemskerk, are masters of this style; and after him Coornhert, one of the best interpreters of his compositions in engravings, must also be mentioned. However much Bruegel follows such examples, with him there is an individual development, differing from the mannerist style, because, in place of the idealizing and sensitive outlines of these artists, he records the figures by means of essentially simple lines, at the same time achieving the modelling of the figures as freely and illusionistically as the mannerists, with lines which follow every movement of the body, cross-hatching and expressive little curves. (See figs. 15-16.)

Internal Factors

HAVING discussed the contemporary influences on Bruegel's draughtsmanship, one must now if one wishes to understand its development and its changes, draw attention to the real inner roots of his drawing. One can best recognize these in the place where the figure is not the prime object of the drawing – in his early landscape drawings. In these the human figure only represents, so to speak, one factor in the movement and life of a section of nature. Here one realizes how far Bruegel has moved from the usual outline drawing, and how he sees people only as belonging to these natural parts of the landscape, bathed in light. Yet his figures are most understandable and effective because they are drawn with a genuine autoplastic rendering of movement, essentially unrealistic and only intuitively created by the juxtaposition of the signs for such movement. True examples of this are perhaps to be found in the group of figures in drawing No. 4, pointing to the distant landscape, where, in order to emphasize forcefully the pointing out of the landscape, the hand of the one shepherd is drawn much too large. Or, in the same drawing, the hindquarters of the horse of the rider who is hurrying away are excessively large in order to emphasize the movement into the distance. In this ability to capture the characteristics and elements of a transitory movement lies a feature of Bruegel's figure-drawing style. Throughout his life he made extraordinarily good use of this gift wherever figures feature in the background of his compositions. It is also characteristic of him throughout his life, that when he was not trying to define a figure by outlining it in pen as in the *naer het leven* studies, he sketched very quickly and modified his drawings as he went along. This is still to be seen in his late work, as for example in the drawing of one of the squires in the *Conversion of St. Paul*, which has become visible under the paint. One sees how here, before he came to the final version in coloured outline and paint, Bruegel drew rapidly and made alterations. In his draughtsmanship – in the pictures, engravings, drawn compositions and of course also in his figure drawings – Bruegel was an artist who did not simply and naïvely copy *naer het leven*. Two examples of this: the quickly executed 'classicist' embroidery with the representation of the elements in *The Adoration of the Kings* of 1564. The second example, and one that will probably be unexpected for many in this context, is the way in which in 1568 Bruegel with simplified and almost childlike draughtsmanship represents the popular broadsheets in the background of *The Peasant Wedding*. (See figs. 21 and 23.)

The Development of His Style of Drawing

With an artist who, even if the surviving *naer het leven* drawings are only the extreme examples of a large number of such studies, approaches his choice of what he wants to represent with such careful thought, it is also natural that there should slowly develop a change of style in his working over of drawings from his sketchbook. The earliest drawings seem to be those connected with the *St. Jerome* of 1553, in which the small figures are still rendered fairly schematically. In these the ink outlines – to emphasize a characteristic trait – seem sometimes to have been roughly corrected. Later, though their modelling remains delicate, the single figures are increasingly executed with these characteristics, and in outline and chiaroscuro. However monochromatic they may seem in the reproduction, it is important to note that they came more and more to be drawn in luminous outline and modelling, with light and dark brown inks. In time, however, everything systematic disappears in his use of hatching. Compared to the drawing of the mannerists the direction and style of Bruegel's line becomes much more individualized, and his method of cross-hatching also brings a totally unexpected, freer life into these drawings. In addition Bruegel, in order to give the vibrant life of the figure bathed in light, makes entirely free use of small curves and twists.

If, in this connection, one looks among Bruegel's dated works for pointers to the dating of individual sheets, it is above all the drawings of the series of *The Virtues* of 1559 which provide genuine connections with the studies. A beggar woman is repeated with great similarity on the sheet depicting *Charitas* (No. 143), and on the same drawing there is also a prisoner for whom a study exists. In all these drawings, which can thus be dated to 1558/59, and in which the figures, though larger than in the first sketches, remain relatively small, the internal drawing is still somewhat summary. Then there follows a further group of drawings. In the early sixties, probably at the same time as the cycle of the small landscapes until about the year 1564, his most delicate *naer het leven* studies were also drawn. In their way they are to be valued as individual works of outstanding artistic importance. In these drawings the secret, silent life of the figures is rendered by means of extremely economical inking in, with sections of the outline in different colours which, in combination with the chalk and sanguine drawing, create a genuine unity. To this group belongs the sheet in Rotterdam (No. 95), the monk from which appears again slightly changed in 1564 in *The Carrying of the Cross* (fig. 24). It is also an important factor of this period that the drawings do not only deal, as has been thought, with the quiet and dull seated peasants and peasant

(25)

women, and the poor helpless beggars, but also increasingly with the transient element of movement, in the search for compositions with the more correct rendering of movement and counter-movement, as in the figures seen from the back. The two woodcutters in Berlin, with the small, rapid sketch of a dancer at the top right (No. 94), are among the most beautiful examples of this.

The *naer het leven* studies with the large figures are correctly considered as the last group of these drawings. This group is generally dated to the late period. But here also a word of caution is needed, for such a beautiful study as that of the horse and carriage with the coachman in the Albertina (No. 105) has, as early as 1558, a parallel in the coachman on the bridge in *Skating outside St. George's Gate* (No. 140). Yet it is right to reproduce this group as a whole, and the principle of their late date counts above all for those drawings in which Bruegel renders his figure studies under the strong influence of the Michelangelesque exaggerated drawing of the figure, like the beggars in Rotterdam (No. 116), or, in my opinion, a drawing at Weimar which has been unrecorded until now (No. 115). One of the very few drawings which was not meant to be a study must also date from this period: *The Painter and the Connoisseur* (No. 126). Here the style of Bruegel's draughtsmanship, which renders so surely the illusion of reality, has also developed the full strength of the dramatization of movement and expression. However, not one of the most perfect of the large figure drawings has survived as a study; one can only get an idea of them if one looks at the forceful and yet absolutely economical mastery of the line in the figures of *The Blind Men* at Naples. In their way Bruegel's *naer het leven* studies are a unique contribution to the understanding of what man looks like, and what he is, in all his poverty and frailty, without regard to appearance and decorum. (See fig. 20.)

Digression on the *Naer Het Leven* Studies

IN order to ascertain which are the authentic drawings by Bruegel, it is also necessary to discover their influence on his followers, and their transformation when copied. There is no doubt at all that, already during his lifetime or very shortly after his death, Bruegel's drawings were so famous that they were continually being copied. The most significant example of this is probably *The Painter and the Connoisseur* (No. 126), the original of which is preserved in Vienna. Even today there are no less than four copies in existence of this drawing. It is a characteristic of these copies that, in their vulgarization of the facial expression and in their simplification of the line, they diverge from each other and, of course, from the original drawing, despite every effort to remain close to it. The existing copies are as follows: 1. The copy belonging to Vincent Korda, London, 298×219 mm., which Tolnay (T. II No. 119) repeatedly put forward as an original (No. A46). 2. The copy by Jacques Savery, which, like Mr. Korda's copy, also shows a larger area; it was formerly in the possession of Dr. Eberhard Kornfeld, Bern (No. A45). 3. Of the same size as the drawing in Vienna is the copy which belongs to Christian Nebehay, Vienna, with the inscription on the back: '*vom Hufnagel 1602*' (No. A47). 4. The coarsest of these variations is the copy in the British Museum, London (No. A48).

An examination of these copies reveals an ever-greater simplification of the line, which is largely due to the failure to understand the significance of Bruegel's subtle draughtsmanship. Even though there is no example of the direct adoption in paintings by Bruegel himself of *naer het leven* studies without any alteration – though inspiration was clearly provided by these – at a later date Bruegel's son, Pieter Brueghel the Younger, made wide use of available paintings and drawings, and he must have possessed a large part of the *naer het leven* studies of his father. His draughtsmanship, despite its similarity in style to that of his father, is always a simplified vulgarization of this. A typical example of such use of known *naer het leven* studies of Pieter Bruegel the Elder is the large water-colour in the Albertina in Vienna (No. A52), in which the horse and carriage (No. 105) and studies of peasants occur. Another example, however, provides an even clearer picture of the son's eclectic methods of adaptation; *The Peasant Dance* by Pieter Brueghel the Younger, which is known through an engraving by Hollar. Pieter Brueghel the Younger's preliminary drawing for it is in London. Large parts of this composition derive from the late painting by Bruegel the Elder, *The Wedding Dance in the Open Air*, in the version at Detroit. For other parts of it drawings exist which represent a more or less successful adaptation of Bruegel's style by his son. They are important because they are evidence of a lost series of further *naer het leven* studies. The group of citizens in the drawing by Pieter Brueghel the Younger has its model in a drawing in Budapest (No. A50), which Meder has rightly already recorded as a copy after Pieter Bruegel the Elder. Much more important, however, is the fact that in a drawing at Besançon (No. A51) there is a group of three men which is also to be found in this drawing, and which has to left and right figures seen from the back, which in their Michelangelesque gesticulation belong to Bruegel's late style. Thus there must have existed genuine prototypes by the father for such drawings, especially as it is clear – as has already been established by Popham – that for the background of this landscape Pieter Brueghel the Younger used the background of the drawing with the *Bee Keepers* (No. 154) by Pieter Bruegel the Elder. Pieter Brueghel the Younger also executed two studies for the painting in the Grisar Collection, which are very closely connected with those of his father. But I consider as most important those drawings by the son in which he has preserved for the future, with partial alterations, compositions by his father. Here the most interesting sheets are the one with *The Epileptic Women of Meulebeeck* (No. A55) and then the studies for the engraved Proverbs Series.

The drawings of the imitators, whether they are considered as works by Pieter Brueghel the Younger, or whether they are anonymous, are always to be recognized by the way in which Bruegel's draughtsmanship and style are uncharacteristically rendered. A typical example of this is the drawing in the Delacre Collection (No. A39), the right half of which repeats a preserved Bruegel drawing (No. 116). To this group of drawings, which in all likelihood are also the work of Pieter Brueghel the Younger, there also belong studies in the same collection, which are connected with the *Wedding Procession*. It is also possible and likely that the drawing of a punchinello in Berlin (No. A40), which has been ascribed to Callot but which Friedländer numbered among the genuine works of Bruegel, belongs to this group. Genuine adaptations of *naer het leven* studies by Roeland Savery have, as far as I have been able to ascertain, not been preserved, and the naming of some drawings as works of Jacques or Roeland Savery has arisen by mistake owing to the fact that these artists inscribed their names on them as the owners of the drawings. In any case the style of the drawings of Roeland or Jacques Savery, with their routine use of the broken outline, and taking into account their etchings, is to be differentiated from that of Bruegel. Of course in the attempt to distinguish between originals and copies there remain some drawings whose attribution is by no means certain, and which can probably only be attributed with certainty as the result of further research. Among such is the drawing in the Louvre (No. A37), with the man pouring out water, which is closely connected with the man in the Proverb Pictures in the Mayer van den Bergh Museum, Antwerp. In the context of the copies it must here be mentioned, although it will be referred to again later, that the drawing in Rotterdam (No. A58) of *The Ascension of Christ*, which Grossmann wants to claim as an original, is at any rate a later copy.

THE COMPOSITIONS

The third group of the surviving drawings of Bruegel comprises the picture compositions. With one exception – the drawing of 1562 of the meeting with a blind man before a village (No. 46) – they are all models for engravings. In contrast to the *naer het leven* studies, it is a group of drawings which Bruegel himself regarded as complete works. Thus almost without exception they are signed and dated. The majority of the surviving composition drawings are designs for engravings of the fifties. Only five can be dated to after 1560. The engravings after these drawings of Bruegel appeared in their first state from 1556 onwards, published exclusively by Hieronymus Cock. If one is to come really close to Bruegel's work one must take far more notice of the engravings than has been done hitherto. Only through them does the whole extent of what Bruegel was aiming to achieve in his instructive and interpretative pictures become clear. More accomplished as works of art are the paintings, and also Bruegel's preparatory drawings, as far as they have been preserved in the original. But it remains remarkable how much genuine forcefulness has been retained, despite the necessary coarsening, in the engravings.

For an understanding of what Bruegel was aiming at in these engravings an exact study of the preliminary drawings is also necessary. Thus in the next section, in addition to pointing out the spiritual and social basis of the instructive and interpretative pictures aimed at the great mass of the urban population, particular attention will also be paid to those features which are important, because the unfalsified originality of his meaning is naturally to be found in Bruegel's own preliminary drawings.

The Style of the Preliminary Drawings

As has been mentioned, the composition drawings are – with only one exception, which is therefore reproduced among the landscape drawings (No. 46) – preliminary drawings designed to be reproduced. Among other reasons this is apparent technically because on some of them clear traces are to be seen of the burin with which the outlines were impressed on the copper plate. Another clue lies in the fact that the inscriptions are in a distinctive handwriting, which is certainly not that of Pieter Bruegel himself, but probably that of a calligrapher, who neatly described the purpose of the sheet, often in a lighter ink than that used for the drawing itself.

If one compares these sheets on the one hand with Bruegel's *naer het leven* drawings, and, on the other, with the landscape drawings, then the following must be said: the outlines of the figures are more strongly concentrated and much firmer than in the *naer het leven* studies; the accentuation of especially important lines has replaced the characterization of the details. Thus, as is their purpose, they remain preliminary drawings for reproductions, and in their inner style they are more tied to the conventions of drawings done as models for engravings than both the earlier groups of drawings. In these drawings much greater use has been made of the tight hatching which is occasionally crossed by diagonals. Though individual figures and sections of landscape in the background may seem free and illusionistic, on the whole these drawings present a bolder and more strongly disciplined impression of depth and space than do the pure landscape drawings. But in these drawings, with their high horizon, the space has become for Bruegel simply an area for action, into which the figures fit as a matter of course. At the least this applies to the drawings and engravings up to about 1561, until when Bruegel's compositions remain purely pictures for instruction and interpretation with a multiplicity of figures, especially in the series of the 'Vices' and the 'Virtues'. In the lavish dispersal over the whole sheet of the most varied figures, people, demons, ghosts, and houses, which, as is fitting for such didactic pictures, seem at the same time to resemble animals, these pictures do, however, show a stronger feeling of unity in all the action than do the direct Netherlandish predecessors of such often satirical compositions, designed to teach the people, of which only two will be named: Lucas van Leyden's large woodcut of the *Cat and Mouse War*, and the sheet with the *Fortunate Ship*, which is also attributed to him. The most closely related precursors of such a realistic universal pictorial stage are, however, the woodcuts of a German artist, who is commonly known as the Petrarch Master, because he executed the illustrations for Petrarch's book 'The Mirror of Fortune and Misfortune.' [The suggestion, almost universally accepted, that this artist is to be identified as Hans Weiditz, is still open to doubt.] In these there has already been created a most effective setting for the action, consisting of more strongly outlined figures, and amongst them sections of landscape, in a freer and more illusionistic style of drawing. (See figs. 19, 22.)

The picture which instructs and demands interpretation (*Lern- und Lesebild*), as seen perfected in the works of the Petrarch Master, belongs to the most characteristic achievements of this new era, in which the representatives of this new learning wanted to teach the people both by means of words and of pictures, and composed pictures of figures which represent particular concepts. Sebastian Brant, the author of the *Narrenschiff*, is already – as has been pointed out by Fränger – a master of such 'Programme Art', which then, starting with the sheets by Dürer, is converted into pictures, and brought to full artistic realization, so that sometimes one forgets the 'programme' or the general meaning, or is only reminded of it later after academic research. In his entire thinking Bruegel follows these examples. If one considers his picture compositions, he belongs to that succession of great Stoic Humanists, who before him, from Petrarch to Erasmus, strove to see the world clearly, without for one moment letting their criticism be limited by a dogma. They all see with open eyes that there is no paradise on earth, and recognize the world for what it is, with all its mistakes. They see the world as something that man must experience, they feel that a deeper faith must exist, which stands higher than any of the dogmatically entrenched Christian creeds. Thus, in order not to lose their inner freedom in these times of religious and social conflict, they find a means of escape in a stoicism, in which, as one can not always have good luck, misfortune is often almost sought after as something good, as a means of purification; and the value of the individual ego in retirement from the world is recognized. This proceeds from a worldly wisdom, which has learnt that one can at least so arrange one's own existence that misfortune cannot do all too much harm, as it has been taken into consideration as something to be expected. On the one hand this creates a genuine freedom – the ability to stand outside the world and to observe human suffering and emotions; it gives the freedom of the conviction that one can see the particular and be saved from a too hasty decision; in short, that one has a grasp of the world, first, trying to study and understand this far more justly, before passing any judgement or sentence. Thus humanism gave man greater personal freedom in all his everyday difficulties, his financial crises and the pressure of foreign occupation, which weighed on the Netherlands at this time. Simultaneously there is a conflict about God, about the meaning of existence, and with this about the supremacy of God. As happens at those times when man, freeing himself from primitive religious ties, dares to look around him, there arises, in addition to the resulting knowledge, the desire to see everything as it really is. Not for nothing does Bruegel belong to the circle of friends of the great geographer Ortelius, who, like

Bruegel himself, strives in his works for an inner, undenominational Christian faith, a faith which in many ways is related to that of the Anabaptists or thinkers like Sebastian Frank, though neither Ortelius nor Bruegel ever officially renounced the Roman Catholic Church. This circle fights for a knowledge of virtue and vice, for recognition of the frailty and sinfulness of man, and for a purer life. Throughout his whole life this is what Bruegel was striving for in nearly all his pictorial compositions. His humanist Christian pictorial surveys are really intended for instruction and interpretation, and in the earliest of the two surviving series, that of the 'Vices', they record exactly all that belongs to such vices. Some of these compositions have inscriptions expressing a very simple, rather coarse morality. It would be nonsense to say of such compositions that Bruegel did not desire to teach and enlighten, or that, in order to do this, he always represented the world pessimistically, as perverse and unreasonable. Today we are often too much fascinated by the artistic qualities of such sheets, and thus tend to look for explanations that are too simple. Something which would normally remain merely commonplace allegory, is mostly given new life and genuine expression by Bruegel. Nevertheless there remains a down-to-earth factor. Not everything in this humanistic programme art is given absolute shape; in a large number of cases, including some of Bruegel's works, the tendency to teach and the conscious moralizing become almost obtrusive. But certainly such works of Bruegel, which he alone signed and executed, are not always completely the result of only his own ideas. What was to be represented in such sheets was probably discussed with friends, such as Ortelius, like the earlier discussions between Sebastian Brant and Dürer or the Petrarch Master.

In all this Bruegel is a man who, while displaying the world before us with all the diversity of its reactions, does not judge it blindly or in hate; but, once he has formed a judgement, he keeps to it. The anecdote which Carel van Mander has passed down to us is characteristic of this. Bruegel had a mischievous and dishonest maidservant. Having caught her telling a lie, he told her that for each of her lies he would make a notch in a stick, and warned her not to continue telling lies for, when the stick was filled, he would throw her out of the house. And this he actually did. Thus in his compositions he shows his theories with apparent objectivity, but in such a way that one has to accept his conclusions. Bruegel is a person who, while upholding a very strict standard for mankind, for as a Christian and a Humanist he believes in virtue and sin, remains human in that he realizes that a certain measure of sin must always be allowed to every man. Bruegel's understanding of the viewpoint of the people, of the way in which they live, and must live in order to be able to exist despite all pressures and predicaments, leads to these moving portrayals. For Bruegel, man is no longer a being who in his innocence is continually threatened by demons, as he is in pictures of the Middle Ages and even still in those of Bosch. He has reached a sort of independence, and with this a new responsibility, extending his thinking. This interpretation makes its first appearance in Brant's *Narrenschiff*. The foolish factor in man is his own tendency to err, from which he has to free himself. His own folly has replaced the threat of the demons.

All this should be borne in mind before those works are discussed in which Bruegel takes into account not only nature and the individual man, but rather the whole world, its light and its dark sides, surveying it with sincerity and freedom. One principle governs all these compositions that instruct and demand interpretation – the word, the idea or the proverb must be converted into the picture. How this happens, and how through this a new, and often unexpected, meaning develops, must be examined. Bruegel achieves his instruction in more than one way; differently in the early sheets than in the later. In the first instance their chief themes are the temptations facing men, and their destruction essentially as a result of their own faults, ranging from greed and stupidity to the gravest sins. The spectator should free himself by experiencing the archaic, though genuine, dread of the world of sin; for the picture contains all the horrors that create this, and these have become plainly visible.

The earliest of such compositions to have been preserved is one in which Bruegel, who could envisage so clearly a landscape with its air and light, concerns himself primarily with the inward and evil elements of life. In the series of the 'Vices' and in the sheets which preceded these, above all *The Temptation of St. Anthony*, he reaches back to a master, as the reincarnation of whom he himself was regarded by all his contemporaries. This is Hieronymus Bosch, in whose work of almost a generation earlier – he died in 1516 – there suddenly stands before us in full reality this uncanny world of demons and of phantoms, which earlier were to be found rather as ornaments in the decorative frames round miniatures. It belongs to the coming of a new era – in our context the world of the Renaissance – that at the moment when man has to fight quite differently for his faith, and is left more to his own devices, there should suddenly spring to the fore the strongly individualized primaeval fears. Such times of crisis are always exceptionally rich in pictures in which horror and dread, terror and oppression, are represented. The vision, and the most life-like and realistic representation, of such a world of horror, is one of the characteristics of the painting of the first half of the sixteenth century. An undiminishing succession of artists keeps the Bosch tradition alive until the time of Bruegel. Bruegel, however, reaches back directly to Bosch, and when Hymans, in the earliest modern Bruegel monograph, put forward the suggestion that a series of preliminary drawings for the engravings after Bosch, which were issued by Bruegel's publisher Hieronymus Cock just at this time, were re-drawn by Bruegel, he was probably right. But Bruegel's draughtsmanship does not resemble the hesitant and dreamlike search and discovery of genuine drawings by Bosch, and is rather characterized by clear outlines and emphasis. In any case Bruegel seeks and finds in Hieronymus Bosch a pattern that is congenial to him, above all where he is concerned with the rendering of terror, fear and horror. On the other hand Bruegel, of whom it is reported by Carel van Mander that he sometimes also liked to terrify in another way with ghost stories, has a different and altered approach to this whole world of misshapen beings and demons than that of Bosch. But one must not go too far here, and must not believe that, because he wanted to frighten others, or sometimes to teach them through such figures, there is no genuine experience behind them, for – compared to those of Bosch – some of his demons are remarkably rationalized. Here Bruegel's own split personality shows itself with convincing and painful clarity – that double ability to be able to experience something and then quietly to give an account of it without being biased. This differentiates the presentation of such demons by a thinker and humanist like Bruegel from that of Bosch. Bruegel, who is rightly praised as a second Bosch, gives to his demon hybrid spirits tasks as bearers of meaning which they could never have had with Bosch. But while Bosch remains the servant of these demons throughout his life, one can see in Bruegel's work that these demons play a rôle only in one element of his experience, the besetting fantasies of fear by day and night; and that then, in the last period of his work after 1564, the world of these misshapen creations of fantasy no longer plays a part in his art. But first the early works must be discussed, in which Bruegel, as far as one can tell from them, sets out to record the world in its reality, with all its vices and virtues, and, of course, also with all its fears.

The basic difference from Hieronymus Bosch is, that Bruegel, far more rational in all his obsessions, had to characterize the faces of such demonic beings. One can not see the whole of Bruegel if one does not observe closely and in detail such faces full of greed and passion, and how these, in order to represent the type of vice, are uncannily joined to animal bodies and limbs, by which the same horror and the same fear of such greed or passion is brought before us. And yet Bruegel places these figures in a natural setting, in which the most remarkable hallucinations and visions have also to be shown. The force of his vision lies in the fact that something which normally is nothing more than a harmless house appears as a wild face. Especially in the series of the 'Vices' is a number of such creations to be found. But here one must be careful, when describing such a world of phantoms, not simply to borrow words from psychology, which do not, in principle, correspond with the phenomenons which are experienced here. In some articles mention is repeatedly made of 'alienation', especially when discussing such compositions of Bruegel. This is a concept which Jasper uses to refer to those forms of delusion in which individual parts of a spectacle attain completely altered meaning, and an overall vision of the object can no longer be obtained. This is never the case with Bruegel, not even in the series of the 'Vices' where the figures are convincingly rendered in their two-facedness together with the sharp and clearly observed hallucinations. It is characteristic of Bruegel, as soon as he knows how to portray the faces of vice more rationally than Bosch, that he, principally wanting to teach, has an essentially more prejudiced and pessimistic vision of the world than Bosch, especially in those demons which personify sexual aberrations. Bruegel frees them of every erotic quality, and they are meant only to rouse disgust. It is also part of Bruegel's essentially pessimistic experience of the world, that he never actually – in a drawing or a painting – tries to depict the sensual beauty of woman.

The series of Bruegel's early drawings ranges from close derivations after Bosch to a completely individual Bruegelesque world of demons. The subject that is represented in any one of these sheets can be basically classified as follows: there are here various pictorial forms for the word which provided the impulse, which in the power of their artistic expression are effective in different ways. In such representations one often finds the re-emergence in the picture of proverbs which arose from examples of reality. Thus there is often nothing more than a modification of normal allegory in popular guise, only comprehensible if one knows the proverb or the word which the picture is meant to illustrate. This is brought to life by humour, as is so much which the cartoonist of today does, and only later, when the actual theme is forgotten, the archaic power of vision breaks through so that suddenly, independent of its theme, the picture has quite a different life. From this it follows that some of these compositions belong to a group of allegories which, because we no longer know their real meaning, do not call forth any immediate and clear-cut reaction. But sometimes, and this is especially true of Bruegel's ghost apparitions, the fear which one tries to laugh away becomes forceful and alive in the picture, which thus receives its own life. The effect of such works differs by degrees; it depends on how far the parts of which such Bosch-Bruegel fantasias are put together are, in general, intuitive in their meaning, how far they are an expression of essentially private and barely ascertainable obsessions, or, in the end, how far they remain only empty pictorial allegories. A good number of these demons are born out of that primitive thinking, where the whole is replaced by the part, as is seen in the picture of feeding, in which by the combination of the two human organs used in eating, the mouth and the arms, which shovel in the food, such an animal of gluttony is created. Such combinations are particularly expressive if parts of the human body are joined together with those of animals. Physiognomically in our primitive experiences certain animal groups are to be identified with certain feelings, especially those of disgust: the slit-eyed fish, the cruel and greedy ineluctability of the many-legged spider. Combined with a human face such features often achieve a convincing vision of gruesomeness. In this world of demons there are also the animal faces, in which both human vice and human feeling are expressed, and those purely intuitive productions and transformations, creations of the lemurs, of the faceless serfs from hell, in which the apparition of the soulless beings withdrawn from the earth is uncannily changed to agonizing fear. All this, often concealed by intellectual whims of the purely didactic picture, is represented in Bruegel's works. His type of vision is essentially different from the demons of a Bosch, or from the largely individualized creatures reflecting sexual fear and mockery in the Rabelaisian French drolleries. Bruegel himself, as far as one can judge from each picture, uses such demons, while remaining at a distance from sensuality, in order to give an entirely frank account of his experiences of fear, greed and suffering. The inner muscular reactions are rendered in that exaggerated dimension with which one experiences them at such moments. From this arise Bruegel's huge bulging eyes of fear, or the exaggerated limbs of greed and grabbing, and finally also the extreme use of his ability to express something by vast magnification, as in the picture of that endlessly stretching snail in the allegory of laziness (No. 136).

Bosch always remains naturally self-conscious in this world of demons, and never stands outside it critically. Thus an uncanny sexual fantasy is evident, especially in his sketches, with all those transformations of the *uccello*, the ancient penis bird (*Penisvogel*), and of the sexual organs, which change into independent living beings and lead their own dull sensuous life. It is no coincidence that it is just these figures of Bosch which belong to those which were adopted by the Italian Venetian artists – by Campagnola – because of their sensuality. Bruegel is more morally embarrassed by such a world. In a deeper sense his demons are not always true visions, they are often too closely bound to his rational imagination. In a way he simply wants to exorcize horror from whole spheres of experience, as in those lemurs with a wide snout, which open up their legs in order to show the sexual organs and the anus at the same time. The last element of pleasure in greed and sensuality, which still lives on in Bosch, has disappeared here. There remains nothing but the mere picture of horror, and Bruegel often repeats the demon which mutilates, wounds or injures itself. A man who has such an attitude towards life, who has to tackle the life of waking and dreaming in this way, will then also suddenly see vices more sharply and more pitilessly, even in all human good nature.

Bruegel's series of the 'Vices' of 1557 and 1558, which is so closely related to Bosch, is completed with a representation of *The Last Judgement* of 1558 (No. 137), which also derives from Bosch in representing without emphasis the border between good and bad, just as in mediaeval pictures, so that the stream of people going to heaven almost crosses into that by which the devils tear people into hell. There are in European art no other examples of such horror pictures which are as all-embracing and as bitter in all their humour and in their portrayal of the vices, as these drawings of Bruegel, and the engravings after them. The next group of the surviving preliminary drawings leads back more into normality, for in the following year, 1559, there begins the series of the 'Virtues', on which Bruegel is still working in 1560. In addition to *The Last Judgement* (No. 137), two preliminary drawings for engravings date from 1558: *Elck* (No. 138) and *The Alchemist* (No. 139), in which Bruegel for the first time expresses his thoughts about the world in large figures. Elck is the man who is always searching with a lantern only externally, that is never within himself, for his ego. He loses himself in his fight with the external world because he lives at strife with himself. The Alchemist is the man who wants to produce gold and riches cheaply out of a thousand recipes, and ends up in the poor-house. Alche-mist – *Alles ist Dreck* ('all is dirt'), as Bruegel himself renders it on the pages of the books in which his doctor studies his black magic. Important as these sheets are for an understanding of Bruegel's thought, artistically they are easily classified. In their draughts-manship they belong to the style of the contemporary satirical sheets, of which examples also exist in the works of other artists, such as Huys and Verbeecq, who were also active in Antwerp. The models for these are probably the large satirical woodcuts of the German artists of the time of the Reformation, such as Beham, Leonard Beck and Amberger. These drawings with large figures also provide the only occasion on which Bruegel comes into contact in one of his compositions with Pieter Aertsen, the great Dutch painter of peasants of this time. And out of this group of drawings, out of this way of seeing men, there developed later the last group of Bruegel's drawings for instruc-tion and interpretation. A continuous series of such compositions – far more than are preserved among the drawings – is available in the engravings.

The next year, 1559, brings the series of the 'Virtues', which shows in what way Bruegel, the judge of man, at once his friend and his critic, sees his virtues. If the model for the background of the vices was the fantastic world of Bosch, which returns once again in the final drawing of this series, in which Christ appears in hell and worlds whirl around each other, then for this world of the virtues the model is the theatre stage with its graduated scenery. One can, for instance, see a direct model for the *Charitas* (No. 143) in Barend van Orley's altar-piece (fig. 26); in principle, Bruegel here builds up his world no differently from the mannerist Heemskerk, only it is more strongly and clearly removed from Italianizing pathos.

The virtues are so pictured that the occurrences which are connected with such a virtue are grouped round the larger allegorical figure of the individual virtue. The series of the 'Virtues' ranges from sheets such as the *Fortitudo* (No. 147), in which the whole rabble of the allegorical animals of vice is destroyed, to that very objectively critical representation of *Justice*, standing there with bound eyes, while all around her 'justice' is being performed (No. 146). All is shown as it actually is, including all the human weaknesses of the profiteers of such virtues. Thus – as Tolnay states – it is wrong continually to speak of a topsy-turvy world in these representations of the virtues, in which the vices actually triumph over the virtues. The final sheet of the series is that of the descent of Christ into Hell (No. 149), in which suddenly that piercing noise again becomes alive for Bruegel, in a vision of the contrast of the world; for in any case Bruegel must always create such visions born out of the fear of sound and of demonically shrill noise, as well as of his pictorial fantasy. As has already been said, the years from 1559 to 1564 were years of crisis, in which Bruegel primarily resists the wicked in his pictures. In this period he made drawings which, as far as one can judge from his surviving work, were the last of his demon drawings, like that of 1564 of the saint destroying the magician and his demons (No. 150). This drawing still belongs to the same world as the slightly earlier painting *Die Dulle Griet*, an allegory of wicked habits, and the picture with the expulsion of the Devil and the demons from heaven. Bruegel leaves Antwerp to settle in Brussels in 1564. This is the time when he marries the daughter of his teacher Pieter Coeck, whom he had held in his arms when she was a child. In 1564, then, as far as one can judge from the surviving drawings and prints, the representations of demons cease. But from the period after this (in Brussels) there dates the series of Christian subjects, only preserved in engravings. Christ as the Good Shepherd, the Way to Emmaus, and then the large close-up pictures of human life. At this time his attitude towards the world undergoes a great change. For until then, if one wants to draw a conclusion from the compositions, he is a man who observes from a distance, and in all his suffering sees life far more detachedly, only very slowly coming face to face with man, who is rather something that merely belongs to life and does not actually signify very much.

In these last years of Bruegel's life there emerged those paintings and drawings in which the human figure is suddenly treated quite differently, predominantly, as something serious and important. Man is so to speak a part of the picture driven more by his own impulses – which is not tantamount to free will – he is rather a victim of his own weaknesses and of his own greed in a world through which the Saviour, unrecognized and yet seen by the masses, had to make His way to the Cross, or the world in which Saul was converted. In this last period of his art Bruegel embraces the Michelangelesque manneristic subjectivism of rendering figures. He now sometimes makes individual expressions so alive that one feels that he is not always in agreement with these poor peasants and their like, and that he has to create works which are suddenly forced to capture such an unwanted, though true, picture, so that one is perhaps not wrong in feeling that in a certain sense Bruegel stands in a position of the strongest criticism of his fellow-man, and is full of despair concerning him.

The last group of drawings, not many in number, shows Bruegel, as far as the style of draughtsmanship is concerned, in close conflict with the prevailing mannerist tradition, as it was represented by the younger generation of academic artists, not only by Frans Floris, but also especially by Stradanus, and then Martin de Vos, whom Bruegel knew personally. But this mannerist expressive emphasis, which was used by this generation of Michelangelo followers around Vasari, regains a much purer meaning in Bruegel's work through the method of his drawing, by which his people are much more successfully characterized as normal everyday beings. In this way the obtrusiveness of such Michelangelesque pathetic gestures is given new meaning, which underlines the burdens of life through the existence of such 'Herculean' peasant figures. Here there is a man at work who uses such methods of expression in order really to bring to life his vision of men in their limitation and in the whole complexity of experience; who has, however, lost at this time that approach to the world of the inquisitive, almost joyful registering of every detail and every diversity, which he had known in his youth. Bruegel must rather record man, quite large and from quite near, poor and lost as he sees him, and as he probably was on the whole at this tragic time of the League of the Gueux. Carel van Mander reports that on his deathbed Bruegel instructed his wife to destroy the most outspoken of his drawings. This was either from remorse, or because he wished to safeguard his wife against punishment. It seems that the round proverbs, which are only preserved in copies, are partially based on works of this period. The very weakly drawn copy after a drawing by Pieter Bruegel of a fool sitting on a broken egg and drinking (No. A54), is dated 1569. It may, of course, be that Bruegel, who started his work at a time in which despite all the oppression there existed a certain degree of understanding and freedom, was a man who knew so well how to observe himself and the world that he became more critical of himself and of the world in these late years, in which the pressure from outside became stronger because of the Spanish oppressors under Alba. This led to that separation in his work between those compassionate Christian paintings, and those others of his closest environment, which, depending on what the spectator himself is, can incite him either to laugh about the world, or can lead to a better insight into its limitations, which Bruegel himself certainly possessed.

LIST OF TEXT ILLUSTRATIONS

Fig. 1. Bosch: *Landscape with owl and song-birds*. Drawing. Rotterdam, Boymans-van Beuningen Museum. (Cf. p. 12.)

Fig. 2. Dürer: *Landscape*. Detail from the "Great Cannon". Etching, 1518. (Cf. p. 12.)

Fig. 3. Martin van Heemskerk: *View of Venice*. Drawing. Vienna, Akademie der bildenden Künste. (Cf. p. 13.)

Fig. 4. Matthys Cock: *Landscape*. Etched by Hieronymus Cock (?). 1543. (Cf. p. 13.)

Fig. 5. Domenico Campagnola: *Heroic Landscape*. Woodcut. (Cf. pp. 13 and 15.)

Fig. 6. Hieronymus Cock: *Small Landscape*. Amsterdam, Print Room. (Cf. p. 17.)

Fig. 7. Cornelis Cort or Hans Bol: *Small Landscape*. Etching. (Cf. p. 17.)

Fig. 8. Master of the Errera Sketchbook: *Small Landscape*. Drawing. Brussels, Bibliothèque royale. (Cf. p. 18.)

Fig. 9. Circle of Bosch: *The Carrying of the Cross*. Detail. Drawing. Vienna, Albertina. (Cf. p. 22.)

Fig. 10. Herri met de Bles: *The Carrying of the Cross*. Detail. Vienna, Akademie der bildenden Künste. (Cf. p. 22.)

Fig. 11. P. Kunst: *Village Musicians*. Rotterdam, Boymans-van Beuningen Museum. (Cf. p. 23.)

Fig. 12. Pieter Bruegel: *The Conversion of St. Paul*. Detail. Vienna, Kunsthistorisches Museum. (Cf. pp. 22 and 25.)

Fig. 13. Bosch: *Beggars and Cripples*. Drawing. Vienna, Albertina. (Cf. p. 22.)

Fig. 14. Hokusai: *Beggars*. Colour Woodcut. (Cf. p. 22.)

Fig. 15. Martin van Heemskerk: *The Torso of the Belvedere*. Drawing. Berlin, Kupferstichkabinett. (Cf. p. 24.)

Fig. 16. Hans Leonhard Schäufelein: *A Lady*. Drawing. Formerly Prague, A. v. Lanna Collection. (Cf. p. 24.)

Fig. 17. Pieter Brueghel the Younger (?): *A Fool sitting on an egg and drinking*. Drawing. London, British Museum. (Cf. p. 35 and Cat. No. A 54.)

Fig. 18. *La pierre levée demie lieue de Poictiers*. Engraving.

Fig. 19. The Petrarch Master (Weiditz ?): *The Battle of the Frogs and Mice*. Woodcut. (Cf. p. 29.)

Fig. 20. Pieter Bruegel: *The Parable of the Blind*. Detail. Naples, Museum. (Cf. p. 26.)

Fig. 21. Pieter Bruegel: *The Peasant Wedding*. Detail. Vienna, Kunsthistorisches Museum. (Cf. p. 25.)

Fig. 22. The Petrarch Master (Weiditz ?): *Sol*. Woodcut. (Cf. p. 29.)

Fig. 23. Pieter Bruegel: *Border embroidered with representations of the Four Elements*. Detail from "The Adoration of the Kings". London, National Gallery. (Cf. p. 25.)

Fig. 24. Pieter Bruegel: *The Carrying of the Cross*. Detail. Vienna, Kunsthistorisches Museum. (Cf. p. 25 and Cat. No. 95.)

Fig. 25. Pieter Bruegel: *The Fight between Carnival and Lent*. Detail. Vienna, Kunsthistorisches Museum. (Cf. p. 22 and Cat. No. 78.)

Fig. 26. Barend van Orley: *The Works of Mercy*. Detail. Antwerp, Museum. (Cf. p. 34 and Cat. No. 143.)

ILLUSTRATIONS TO THE TEXT

Fig. 1. Bosch: LANDSCAPE WITH OWL AND SONG-BIRDS. Drawing. Rotterdam,
Boymans-van Beuningen Museum.

Fig. 2. Dürer: LANDSCAPE. Detail from the "Great Cannon". Etching, 1518.

Fig. 3. Martin van Heemskerk: VIEW OF VENICE. Drawing. Vienna, Akademie der Bildenden Künste.

Fig. 4. Matthys Cock: LANDSCAPE. Etched by Hieronymus Cock (?). 1543.

Fig. 5. Domenico Campagnola: HEROIC LANDSCAPE. Woodcut.

Fig. 6. Hieronymus Cock: SMALL LANDSCAPE. Amsterdam, Print Room.

Fig. 7. Cornelis Cort or Hans Bol: SMALL LANDSCAPE. Etching.

Fig. 8. Master of the Errera Sketchbook: SMALL LANDSCAPE. Drawing. Brussels, Bibliothèque Royale.

Fig. 9. Circle of Bosch: THE CARRYING
OF THE CROSS. Detail. Drawing.
Vienna, Albertina.

Fig. 10. Herri met de Bles: THE CARRYING OF THE CROSS.
Detail. Vienna, Akademie der Bildenden Künste.

Fig. 11. P. Kunst: VILLAGE MUSICIANS. Rotterdam,
Boymans-van Beuningen Museum.

Fig. 12. Pieter Bruegel:
THE CONVERSION OF ST. PAUL. Detail.
Vienna, Kunsthistorisches Museum.

Fig. 14. Hokusai: BEGGARS. Colour Woodcut.

Fig. 13. Bosch: BEGGARS AND CRIPPLES. Drawing. Vienna, Albertina.

Fig. 16. Hans Leonhard Schäufelein: A LADY. Drawing.
Formerly Prague, A. v. Lanna Collection.

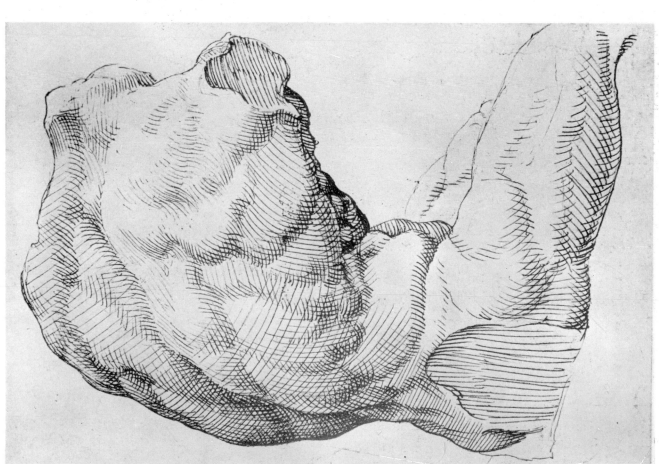

Fig. 15. Martin van Heemskerk: THE TORSO OF THE BELVEDERE.
Drawing. Berlin, Kupferstichkabinett.

Fig. 17. Pieter Brueghel the Younger (?):
A Fool Sitting on an Egg and Drinking.
Drawing. London, British Museum.
(Cat. No. A 54).

Fig. 18. La pierre levée demie lieue de Poictiers.
Engraving.

Fig. 19. Petrarch Master (Weiditz ?): The Battle of the Frogs and Mice. Woodcut.

Fig. 20. Pieter Bruegel: THE PARABLE OF THE BLIND. Detail. Naples, Museum.

Fig. 21. Pieter Bruegel: THE PEASANT WEDDING. Detail. Vienna, Kunsthistorisches Museum.

Fig. 22. Petrarch Master (Weiditz ?): SOL. Woodcut.

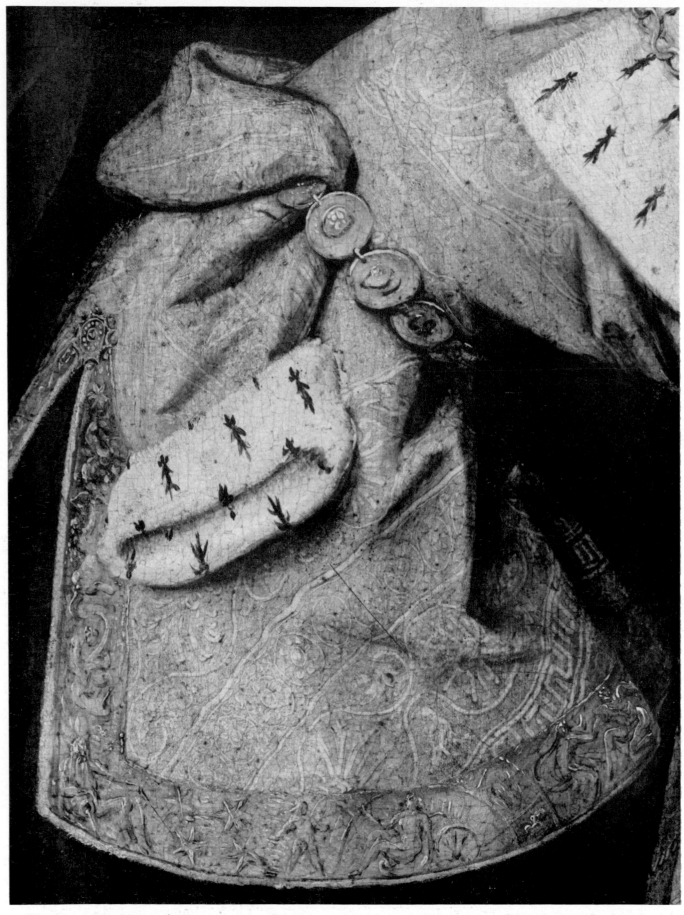

Fig. 23. Pieter Bruegel: Border embroidered with Representations of the Four Elements.
Detail from "The Adoration of the Kings". London, National Gallery.

Fig. 24. Pieter Bruegel: THE CARRYING OF THE CROSS. Detail. Vienna, Kunsthistorisches Museum.

Fig. 25. Pieter Bruegel: THE FIGHT BETWEEN CARNIVAL AND LENT. Detail. Vienna, Kunsthistorisches Museum.

Fig. 26. Barend van Orley: THE WORKS OF MERCY. Detail. Antwerp, Museum.

THE PLATES

DRAWINGS REPRODUCED IN THE ORIGINAL SIZE

ARE MARKED WITH AN ASTERISK (*)

THE DRAWINGS OF PIETER BRUEGEL

I : LANDSCAPES

*I: Cat. No. 1. RIVER VALLEY WITH MOUNTAIN IN BACKGROUND. Dated 1552. Paris, Louvre

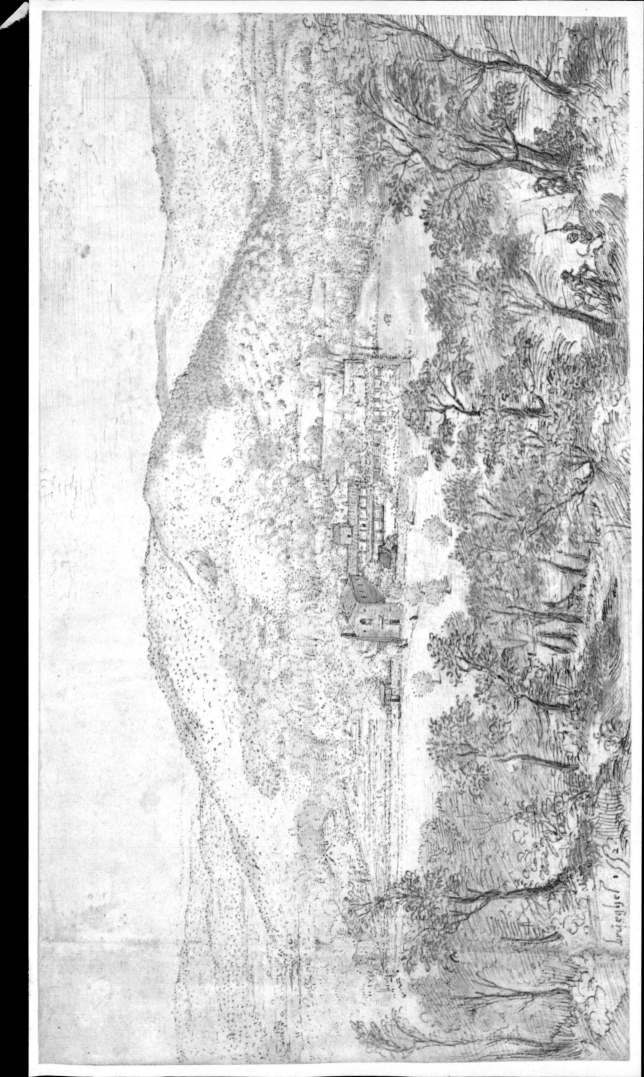

3: Cat. No. 3. Landscape with Walled Town. Dated 1553. London, British Museum

4: Cat. No. 4. LANDSCAPE WITH RIVER AND MOUNTAINS. Dated 1553. London, British Museum

5: Cat. No. 5. ALPINE LANDSCAPE. Dated 1553. Paris, Louvre

6: Cat. No. 6. Landscape with Rocky Mountains. About 1553. Dresden, Kupferstichkabinett

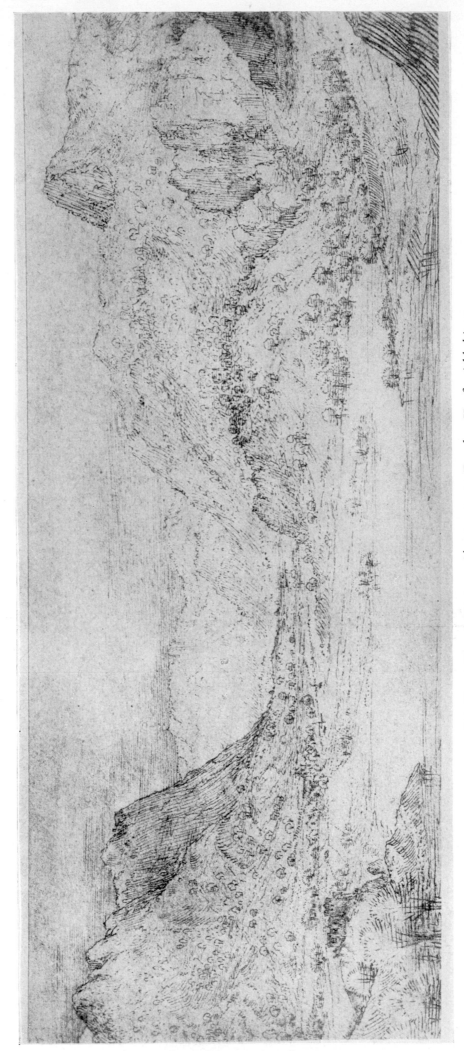

7: Cat. No. 7. RIVER VALLEY. About 1553–54. Dresden, Kupferstichkabinett

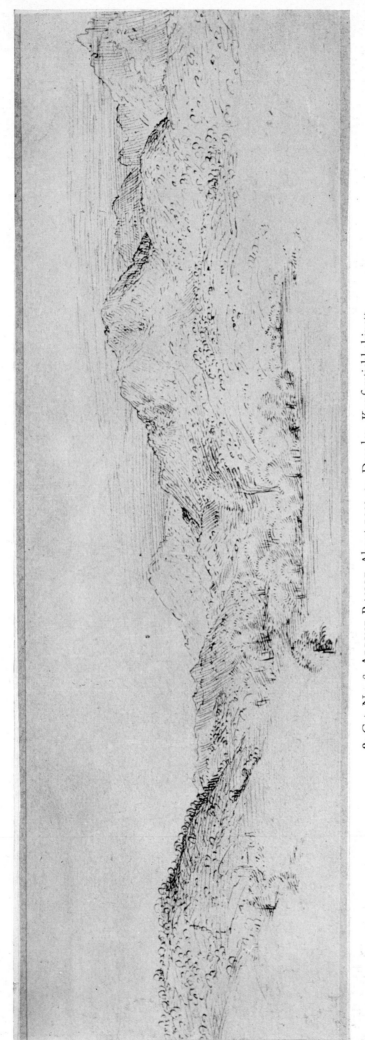

8: Cat. No. 8. Alpine Range. About 1553–54. Dresden, Kupferstichkabinett

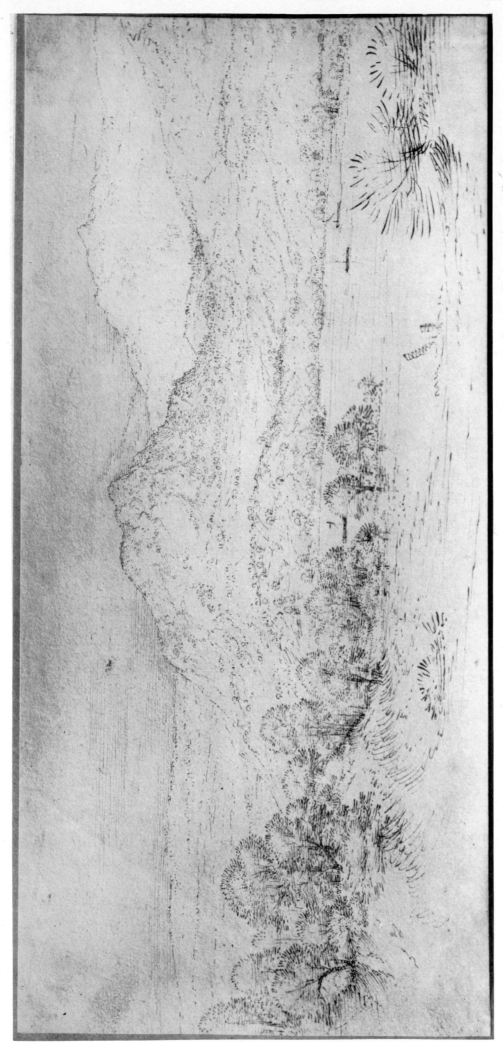

9: Cat. No. 9. Landscape with River Valley and Mountains of Medium Height. Chatsworth, Devonshire Collection

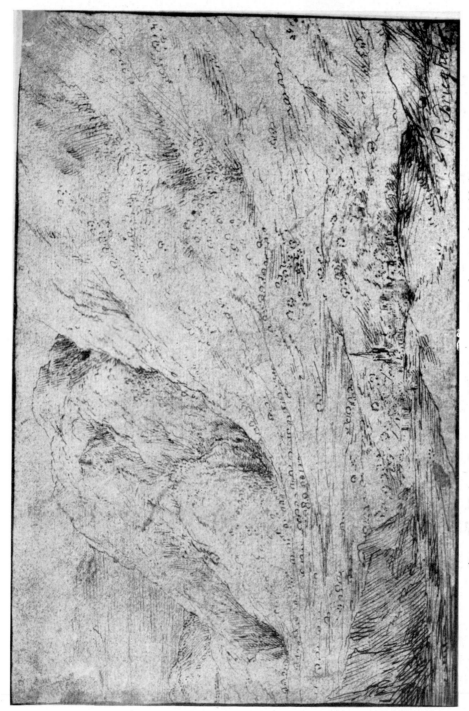

*10: Cat. No. 10. GIGANTIC MOUNTAINS. Dresden, Kupferstichkabinett

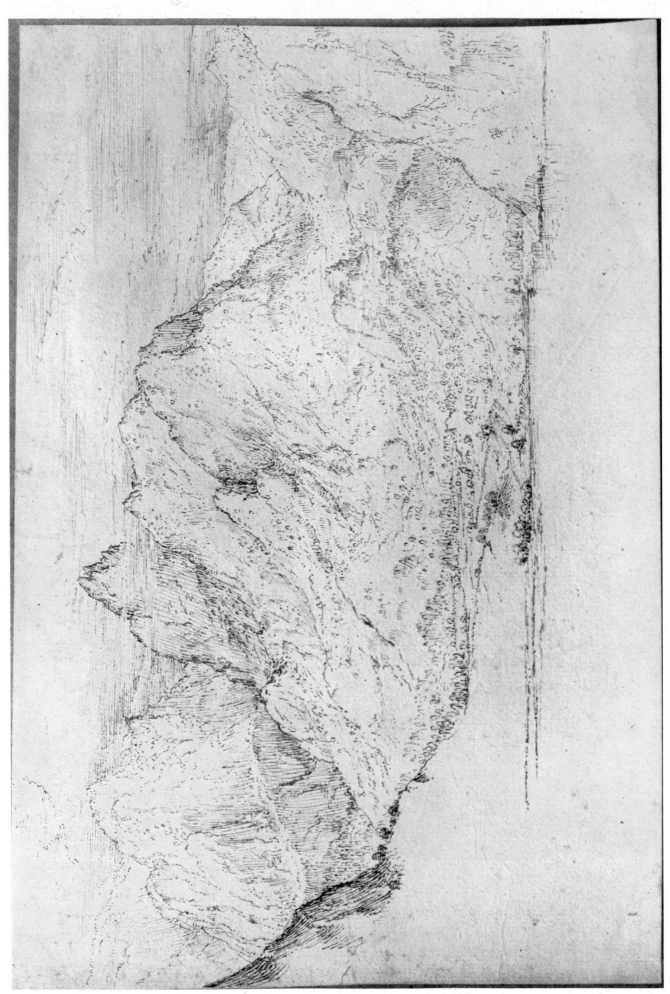

*II: Cat. No. 11. Landscape with Range of Mountains. Chatsworth, Devonshire Collection

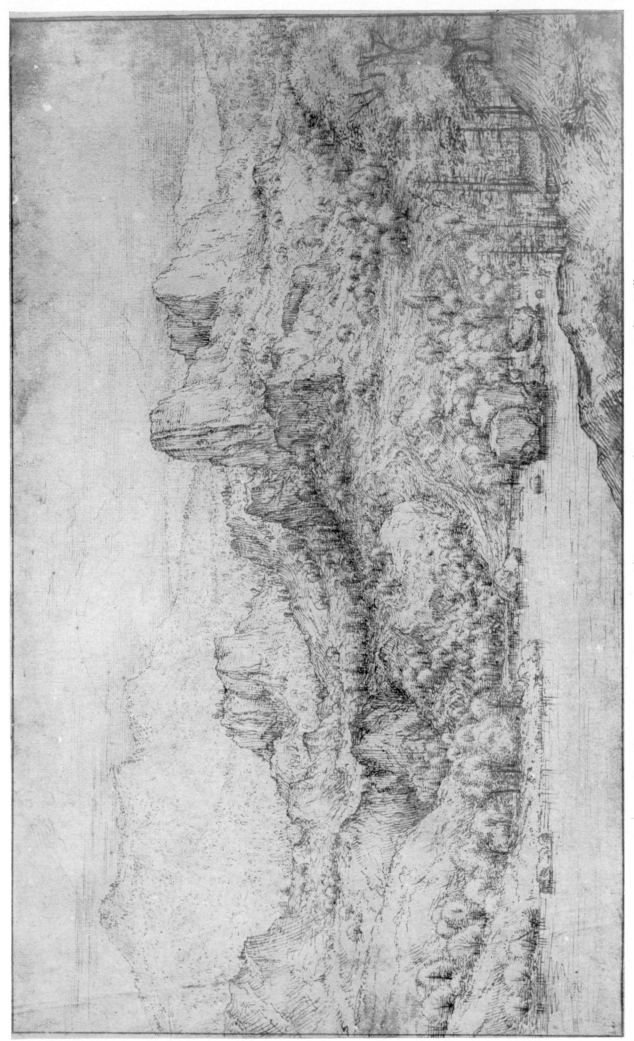

12: Cat. No. 12. ALPINE LANDSCAPE. About 1555–56. London, Count Antoine Seilern Collection

13: Cat. No. 13. Mountain Ravine. Dated (15)55. Paris, Louvre

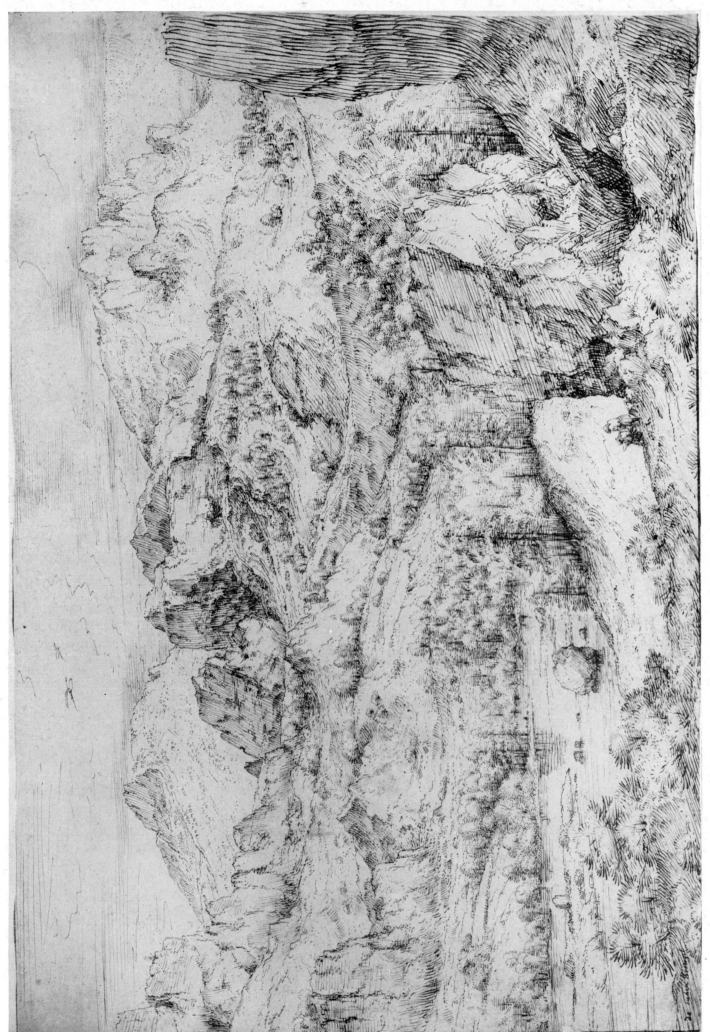

14: Cat. No. 14. Alpine Landscape with an Artist Sketching. About 1555–56 (?). London, Count Antoine Seilern Collection

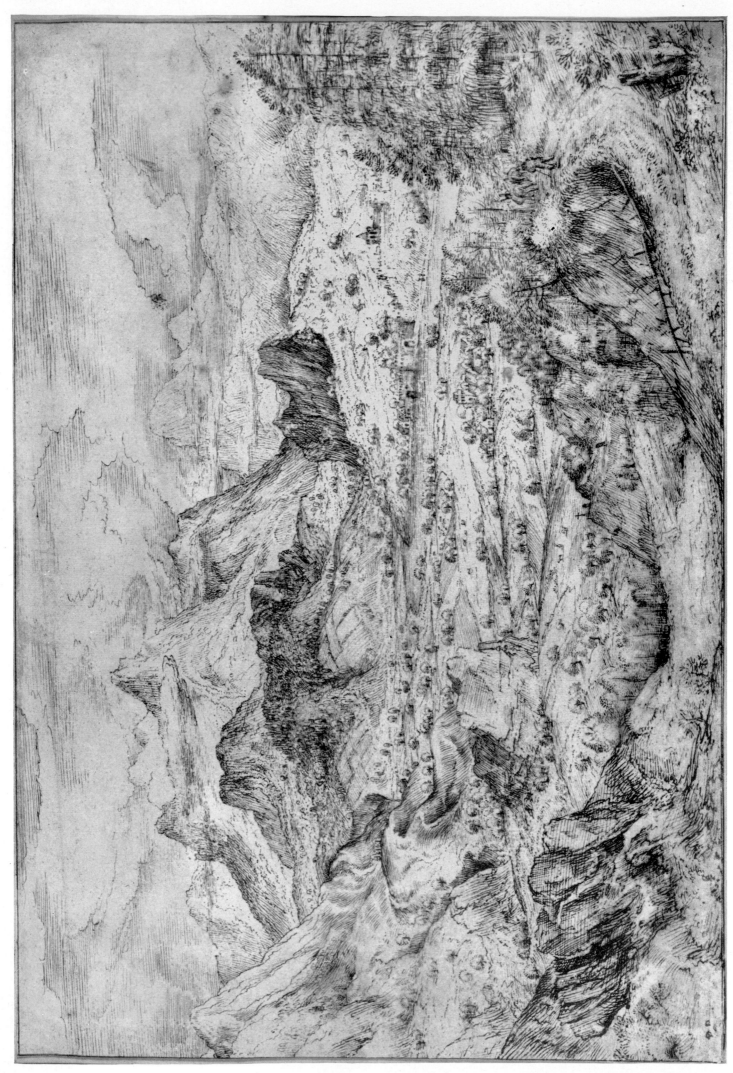

16: Cat. No. 16. LANDSCAPE WITH RANGE OF MOUNTAINS. Dated 1556. Chatsworth, Devonshire Collection

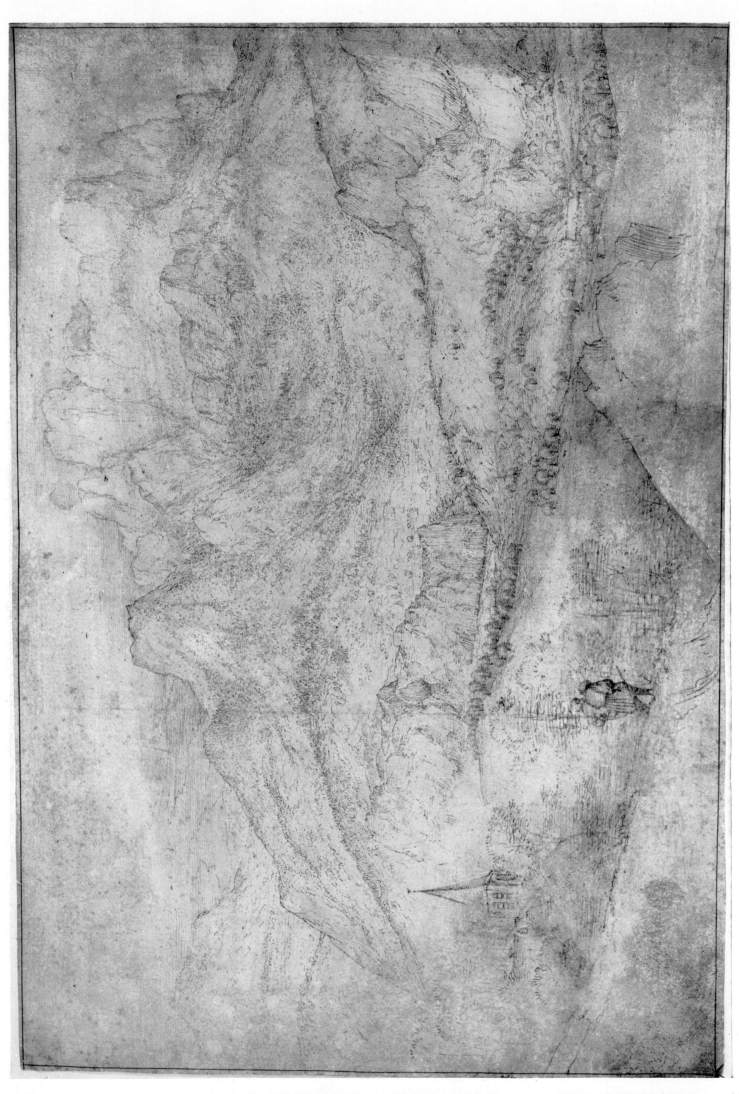

17: Cat. No. 18. Alpine Landscape. About 1556. Cambridge, Mass., Fogg Art Museum

18: Cat. No. 21. THE LARGE RHINE LANDSCAPE. About 1553–54. New York, Pierpont Morgan Library

19: Cat. No. 19. VIEW OF WALTERSSPURG. About 1553–54. Brunswick, Maine, Bowdoin College Museum of Fine Arts

20: Cat. No. 20. MOUNTAIN LANDSCAPE WITH FIR TREE AND A CROSS IN LEFT FOREGROUND. About 1553–1554.
Rotterdam, Boymans-van Beuningen Museum

21: Cat. No. 22. Landscape with Town and St. Jerome. Dated (1)553. Zurich, Dr. Felix Somary Collection

22: Cat. No. 25. Sea Landscape with Rocky Island and an Italian-Style Cloister; the Holy Family in the Foreground. About or after 1559.
Berlin, Kupferstichkabinett

23: Cat. No. 24. Landscape with Two Horsemen. (Verso of Plate 24.) About 1554 (?). 329 × 466 mm. Berlin, Kupferstichkabinett

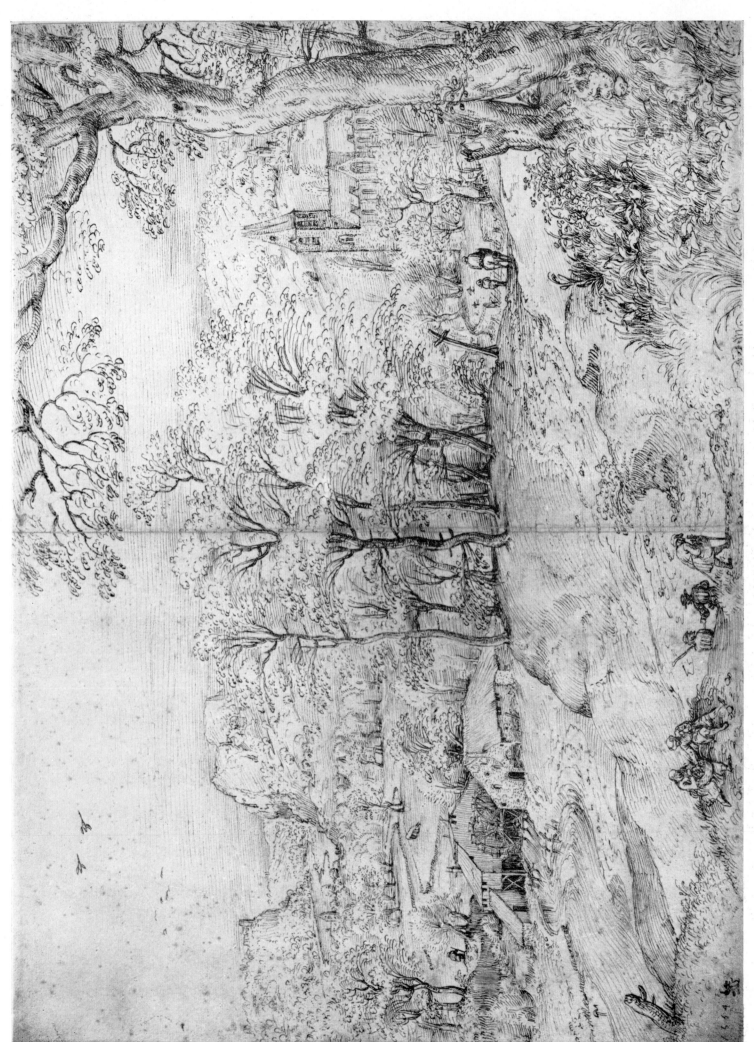

24: Cat. No. 23. Large Landscape with Trees and a Church. Dated 1554. Berlin, Kupferstichkabinett

*26: Cat. No. 27. ROCKY LANDSCAPE WITH CASTLE AND RIVER VALLEY. Dated 1559. Vienna, Akademie der bildenden Künste

27: Cat. No. 28. Mountain Landscape with Narrow Path between Rocks, and River Valley. Dated 1560. Berlin, Kupferstichkabinett

28: Cat. No. 29. River Landscape with Large Rocks at Left, and a Sailing Boat. Dated 1560. Berlin, Kupferstichkabinett

*29: Cat. No. 30. ROCKY RIVER LANDSCAPE. Dated 1560. Amsterdam, Rijksmuseum

30: Cat. No. 31. ROCKY LANDSCAPE. Dated 1560. Paris, F. Lugt Collection

31: Cat. No. 32. Rocky Landscape with a Castle. Dated 1560. London, Count Antoine Seilern Collection

32: Cat. No. 33. Landscape with Castle on Hill to the Right. About 1560. Berlin, Kupferstichkabinett

33: Cat. No. 34. VILLAGE LANDSCAPE WITH PEASANTS AND A TREE. Dated 1560.
London, Count Antoine Seilern Collection

34: Cat. No. 35. VILLAGE LANDSCAPE WITH PEASANT FAMILY IN THE FOREGROUND. Dated 1560.
Vienna, Akademie der bildenden Künste

35: Cat. No. 36. Landscape with a Village and a Family Walking in the Foreground. Dated 1560.
Paris, Louvre

36: Cat. No. 37. Village Landscape with Church in the Foreground. Dated 1560.
Berlin, Kupferstichkabinett

37: Cat. No. 38. CASTLE WITH ROUND TOWERS, AT THE LEFT A RIVER. Dated 1561. Berlin, Kupferstichkabinett

38: Cat. No. 39. LANDSCAPE WITH RUINED CASTLE AND ROCKY GATEWAY. Dated 1561. Vienna, Albertina

*39: Cat. No. 40. Ruined Castle and Chapel on Rocky Hill. Dated 1561. Berlin, Kupferstichkabinett

*40: Cat. No. 41. Sunrise Over a Valley. Dated 1561. Paris, Louvre

41: Cat. No. 42. WILDERNESS OF ROCKS WITH GORGE AND CASTLE. Dated 1561. Rotterdam, Boymans-van Beuningen Museum

42: Cat. No. 43. Landscape with a Castle. Dated 1561. Besançon, Musée des Beaux-Arts

43: Cat. No. 44. ROCKY LANDSCAPE WITH FORTRESS-CASTLE AT THE LEFT. Dated 1562. Munich, Kupferstichkabinett

44: Cat. No. 45. Landscape with a Village. Dated 1562. Brunswick, Herzog Anton Ulrich Museum

45: Cat. No. 46. THE BLIND MEN. Dated 1562. Berlin, Kupferstichkabinett

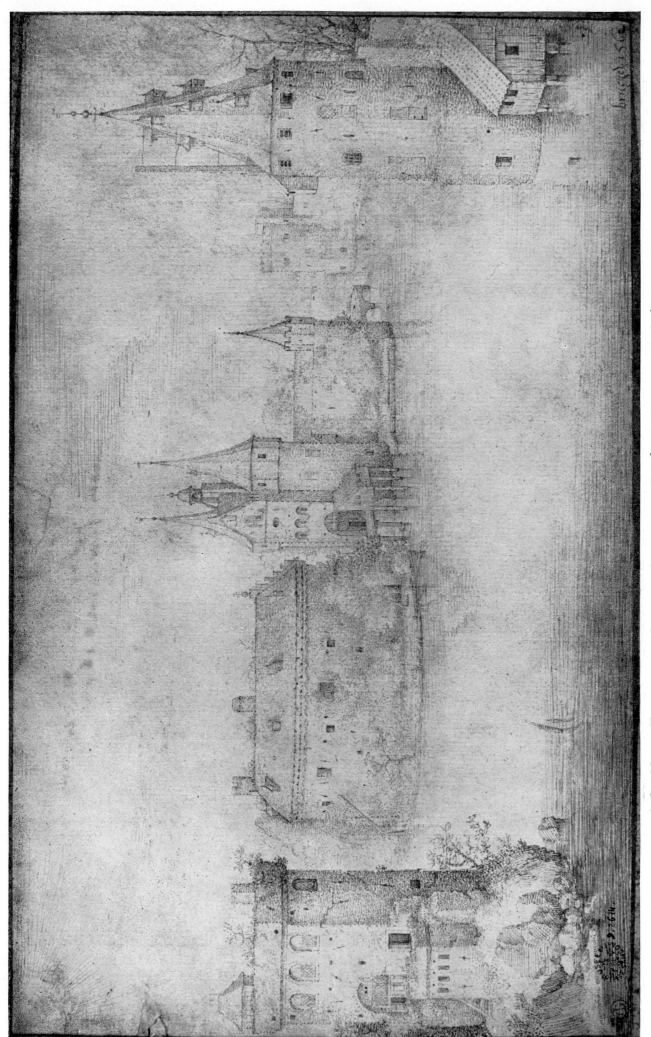

46: Cat. No. 47. Towers and Gates of Amsterdam. Dated 1562. Besançon, Musée des Beaux-Arts

47: Cat. No. 48. TOWERS AND GATES OF AMSTERDAM. Dated 1562. Besançon, Musée des Beaux-Arts

48: Cat. No. 49. Towers and Gates of Amsterdam. Dated 1562. Boston, Mass., Museum of Fine Arts

49: Cat. No. 50. Marine Landscape with a View of Antwerp in the Background. London, Count Antoine Seilern Collection

II: "NAER HET LEVEN"

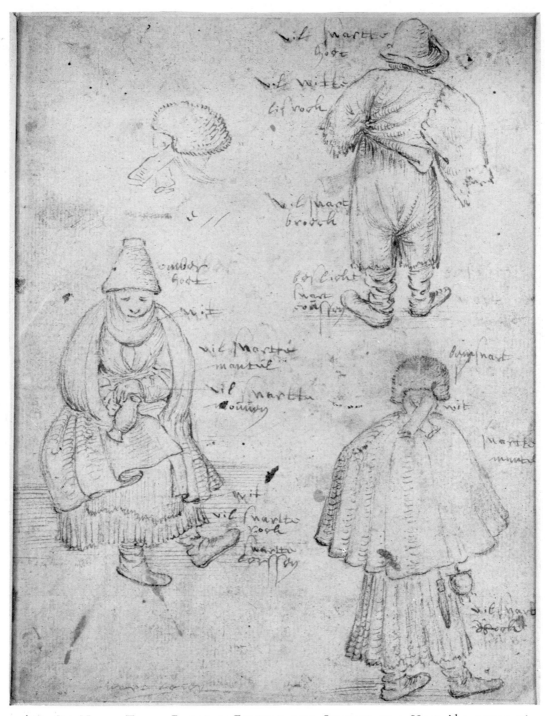

*50: Cat. No. 51. Three Peasant Figures and Sketch of a Hat. About 1553–56.
Berlin, Kupferstichkabinett

*51: Cat. No. 54. Burgher Seen from the Back. Berlin, Kupferstichkabinett

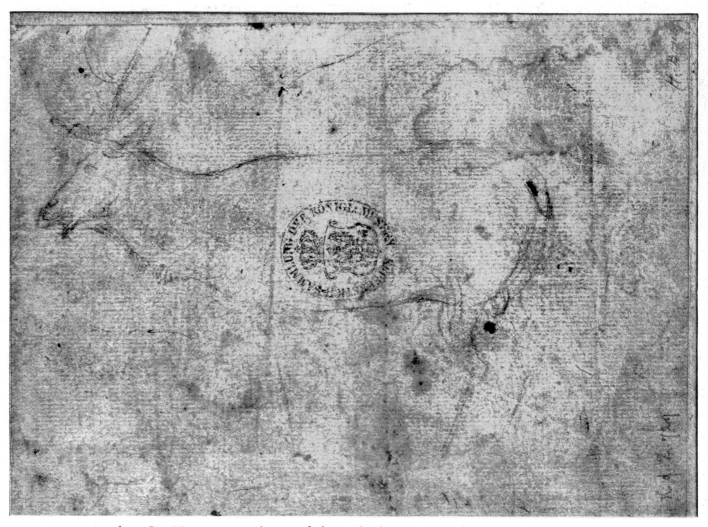

*52: Cat. No. 52. S TAG. (Verso of Plate 50.) About 1553. Berlin, Kupferstichkabinett

***53**: Cat. No. 53. Buffalo. (Verso of Plate 51.) Berlin, Kupferstichkabinett

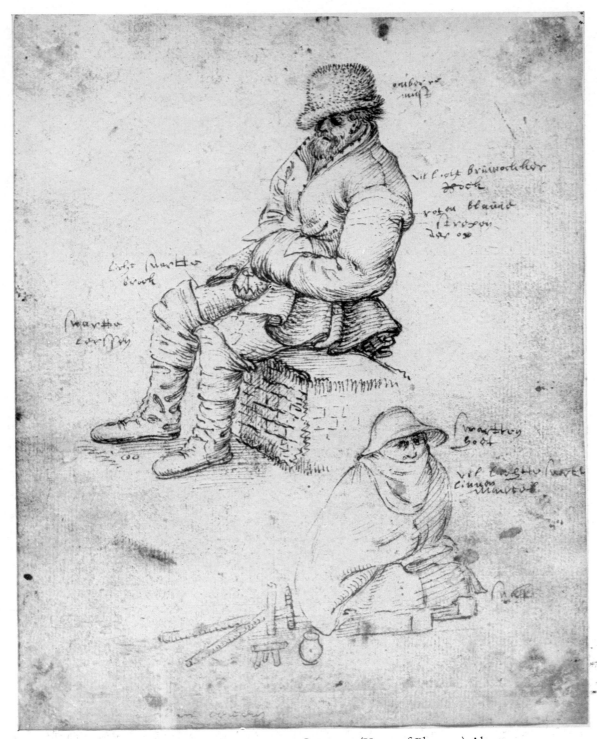

*54: Cat. No. 55. SEATED BURGHER AND CRIPPLE. (Verso of Plate 55.) About 1553–55.
London, Count Antoine Seilern Collection

*55: Cat. No. 56. SEATED BURGHER. About 1553–55. London, Count Antoine Seilern Collection

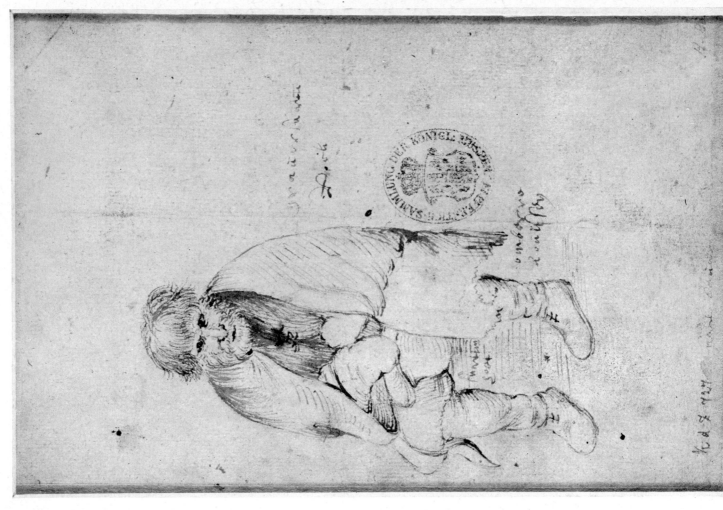

*57: Cat. No. 58. SEATED PEASANT SEEN FROM THE FRONT. (Verso of Plate 56.)
About 1558. Berlin, Kupferstichkabinett

*56: Cat. No. 57. WALKING PEASANT WITH HOE ON HIS SHOULDER. After 1556 – about 1558.
Berlin, Kupferstichkabinett

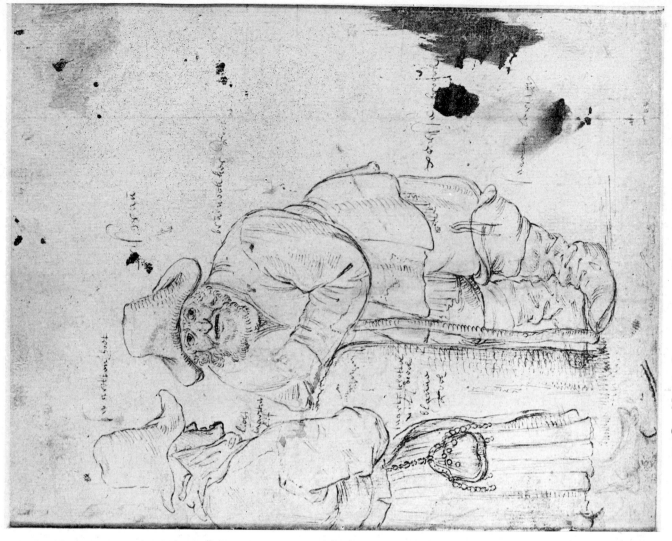

59: Cat. No. 60. PEASANT AND PEASANT WOMAN. About 1558.
Berlin, Kupferstichkabinett

58: Cat. No. 59. TWO MARKET WOMEN. (Verso of Plate 59.) About 1558.
Berlin, Kupferstichkabinett

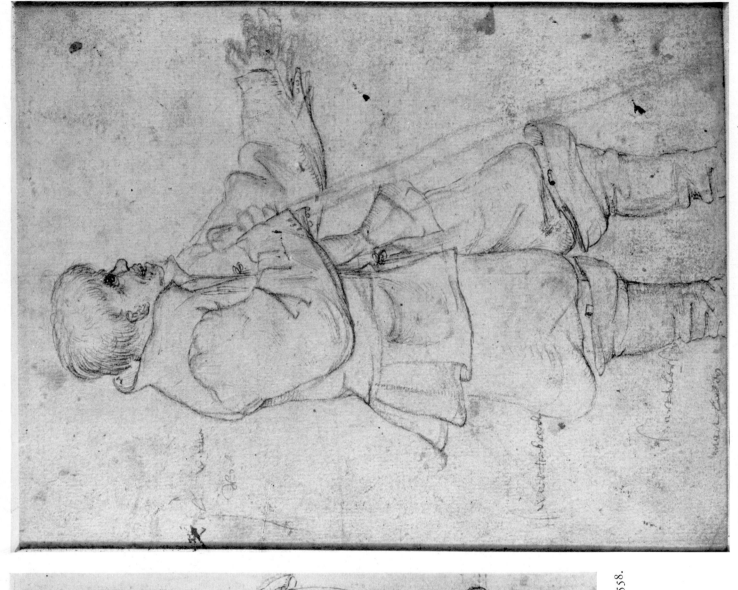

*63: Cat. No. 63. Market Woman Seen from the Front.
(On the verso of Plate 61.) About 1558–59.
Berlin, Kupferstichkabinett

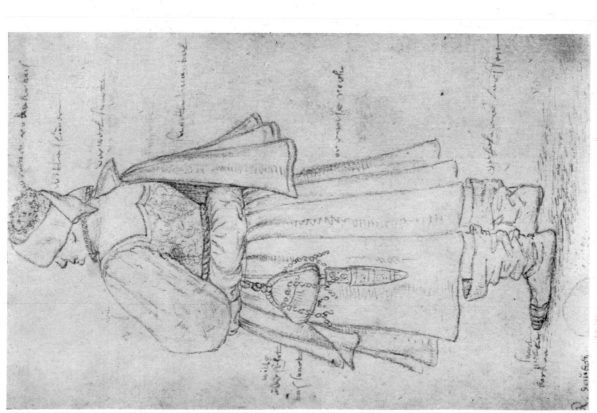

*62: Cat. No. 66. Rich Peasant Woman Seen in
Three-Quarter Profile. About 1559.
The Hague, Le Clerq Collection

'65': Cat. No. 65. Peasant Woman with a Milk Jug.
About 1558–59. Berlin, Kupferstichkabinett

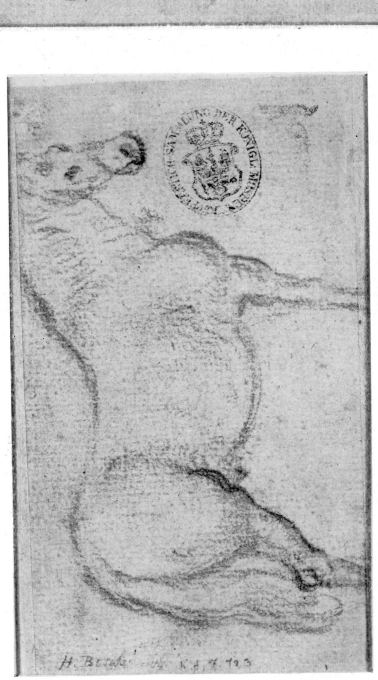

'64': Cat. No. 64. Study of a Horse. (Verso of Plate 65.) About 1558–59. Berlin, Kupferstichkabinett

*67: Cat. No. 68. Standing Man with an Axe under his Arm,
Seen from the Back. (Verso of Plate 66.) About 1558–59.
Frankfurt-am-Main, Städelsches Kunstinstitut

*66: Cat. No. 67. Standing Market Woman Seen from the
Back. About 1558–59. Frankfurt-am-Main, Städelsches Kunstinstitut

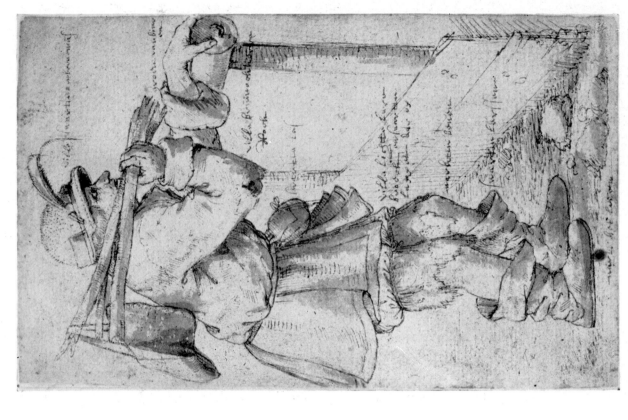

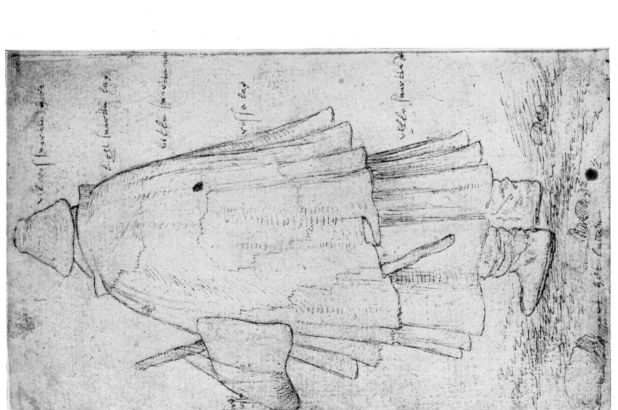

*69: Cat. No. 70. Peasant Seen in Profile, his Left Hand on a Wooden Fence. (Verso of Plate 68.) About 1558–60. Portinscale, Cumberland, F. Springell Collection

*68: Cat. No. 69. Figure Enveloped in a Padded Cloak, Seen from the Back. About 1558–60. Portinscale, Cumberland, F. Springell Collection

*71: Cat. No. 72. Walking Man Enveloped in a Cloak. About 1559–63. Frankfurt-am-Main, Städelsches Kunstinstitut

*70: Cat. No. 71. Figure in a Ragged Cloak. (Verso of Plate 71.) About 1559–63. Frankfurt-am-Main, Städelsches Kunstinstitut

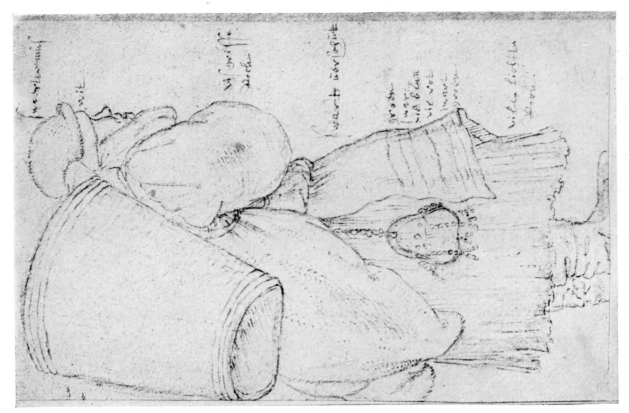

*73: Cat. No. 74. Peasant Woman with Basket. Seen in Quarter Profile. (Verso of Plate 72.) About 1559–63. Stockholm, National Museum

*72: Cat. No. 73. Peasant Woman with Hoe and Basket. About 1559–63. Stockholm, National Museum

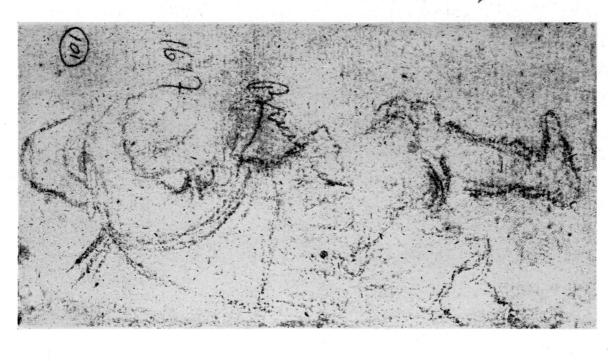

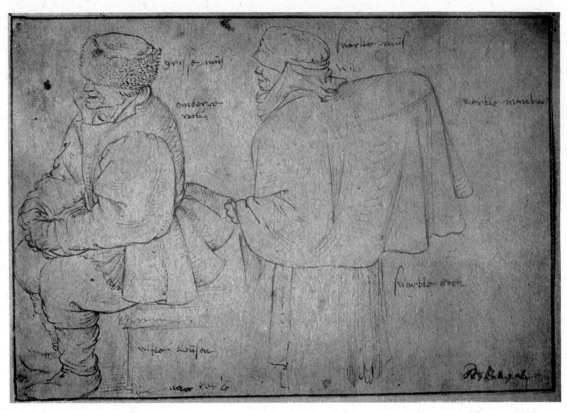

*76: Cat. No. 77 SEATED PEASANT, AND STANDING PEASANT WOMAN WITH BASKET ON
HER BACK. About 1559. New Rochelle, N.Y., Curtis O. Baer Collection

*77: Cat. No. 79. THREE PEASANT FIGURES, TWO SEEN FROM THE BACK, ONE IN PROFILE. About 1559–63.
Stockholm, National Museum

*78: Cat. No. 80. A Seated and a Standing Peasant. About 1559–63. Berlin, Kupferstichkabinett

*79: Cat. No. 81. Peasant Seen from the Back and Soldier Seen in Three-Quarter Profile About. 1559–63.
Berlin, Kupferstichkabinett

*80: Cat. No. 82. THREE PEASANT FIGURES. After 1560. Formerly Paris, Heseltine-Richter Collection

*81: Cat. No. 83. Two Figures in Hungarian Costume. About 1559–63. Berlin, Kupferstichabinett

*82: Cat. No. 84. Three Studies, on the Left a Cripple, on the Right a Soldier. After 1560.
Rotterdam, Boymans-van Beuningen Museum

*83: Cat. No. 85. THREE STUDIES, IN THE CENTRE A SEATED BEGGAR SEEN IN PROFILE. About 1563–64.
Rotterdam, Boymans-van Beuningen Museum

*84: Cat. No. 86. CRIPPLED BEGGAR. About 1563.
Amsterdam, Rijksmuseum

*85: Cat. No. 88. Burgher Seen from the Back. After 1564.
Vorden (Huize de Wiersse), Mme Gatacre-de Stuers

*86: Cat. No. 89. FOUR MEN STANDING IN CONVERSATION. About 1560–63. Paris, Louvre

*87: Cat. No. 90. THE SHEPHERD. About 1560–63. Dresden, Kupferstichkabinett

*88: Cat. No. 91. Two Burghers Seen from the Back. About 1564.
Brussels, Bibliothèque Royale

*90: Cat. No. 93. Young Peasant Seen from the Back and Older Peasant in Half-Length.
About 1564–65 Formerly Vienna, Liechtenstein Collection

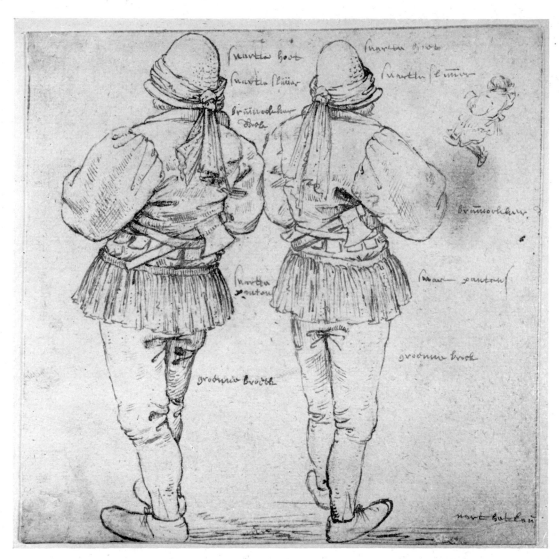

*93: Cat. No. 96. PEASANT YOUTH SEEN FROM THE BACK. 1564. Rotterdam, Boymans-van Beuningen Museum

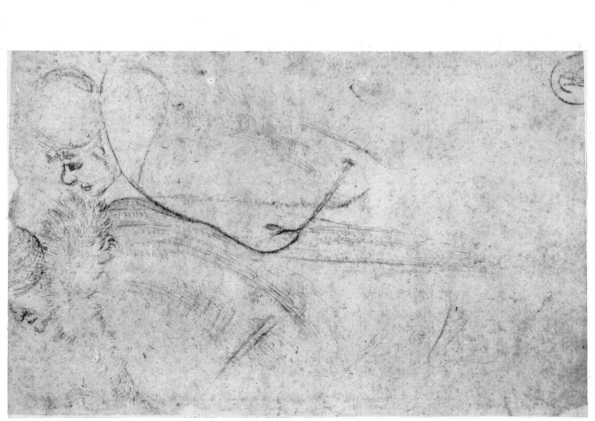

*92: Cat. No. 95. TWO SPECTATORS. (Verso of Plate 93.) 1564. Rotterdam, Boymans-van Beuningen Museum

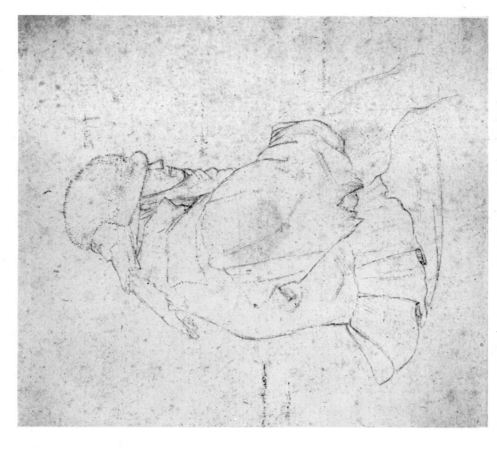

*95: Cat. No. 98. Seated Old Peasant Woman Seen in Profile. About 1564. Rotterdam, Boymans-van Beuningen Museum

*94: Cat. No. 97. Two Market Women. About 1564. Rotterdam, Boymans-van Beuningen Museum.

*96: Cat. No. 100. An Old Miner. About 1564.
Stockholm, National Museum

*97: Cat. No. 99. The Blind Beggar.
About or after 1564. Dresden, Kupferstichkabinett

*98: Cat. No. 101. Two Mountain Peasants. About 1564. Berlin, Kupferstichkabinett

99: Cat. No. 102. THE PILGRIM. About 1564. Vorden (Huize de Wiersse), Mme Gatacre-de Stuers

*100: Cat. No. 103. Two Burghers Seen in Profile. About 1564. Zürich, Private Collection

*101: Cat. No. 104. THREE STUDIES OF PEASANTS. About 1564. Formerly Berlin, Kupferstichkabinett

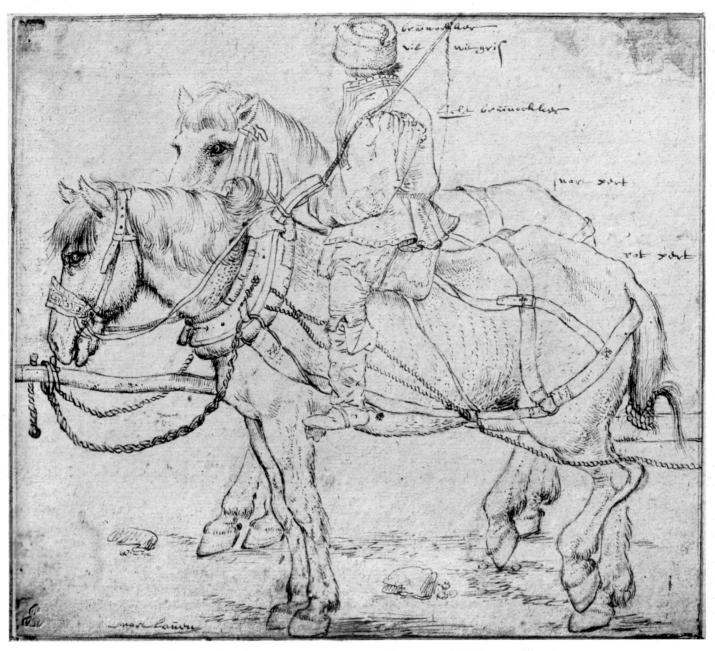

*102: Cat. No. 105. TEAM OF HORSES. About 1564 (?). Vienna, Albertina

*103: Cat. No. 107. PEASANT SEEN FROM THE BACK. (Verso of Plate 104.)
1564 or later. London, Count Antoine Seilern Collection

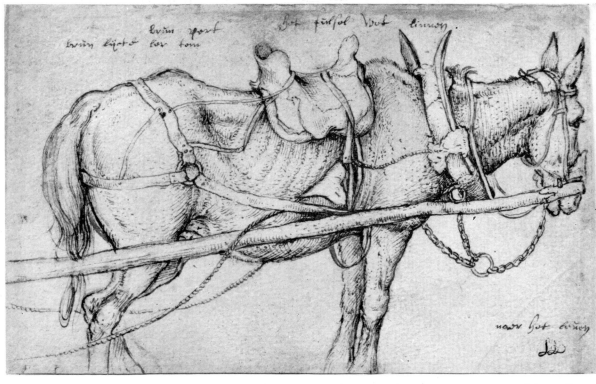

*104: Cat. No. 106. A MULE IN HARNESS. About 1564 or later. London, Count Antoine Seilern Collection

*105: Cat. No. 108. The 'Horse-Trader'. About 1563. Frankfurt-am-Main, Städelsches Kunstinstitut

*106: Cat. No. 109. Three Burghers, One Seen in Profile, One from the Back, and One in Three-Quarter View. About 1563. Vorden (Huize de Wiersse), Mme Gatacre-de Stuers

*107: Cat. No. 110. Two Rabbis. About 1563–64. Frankfurt-am-Main, Städelsches Kunstinstitut

*109: Cat. No. 112. Walking Man. About 1564. Frankfurt-am-Main, Städelsches Kunstinstitut

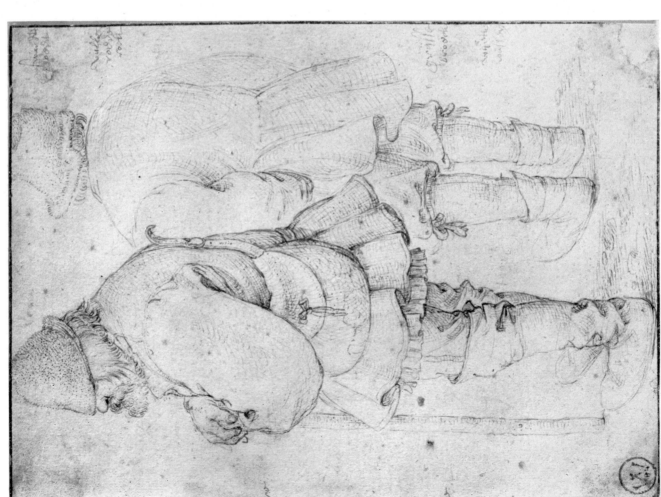

*108: Cat. No. 111. Two Peasants, one in Profile, the other Seen from the Back. After 1564. Rotterdam, Boymans-van Beuningen Museum

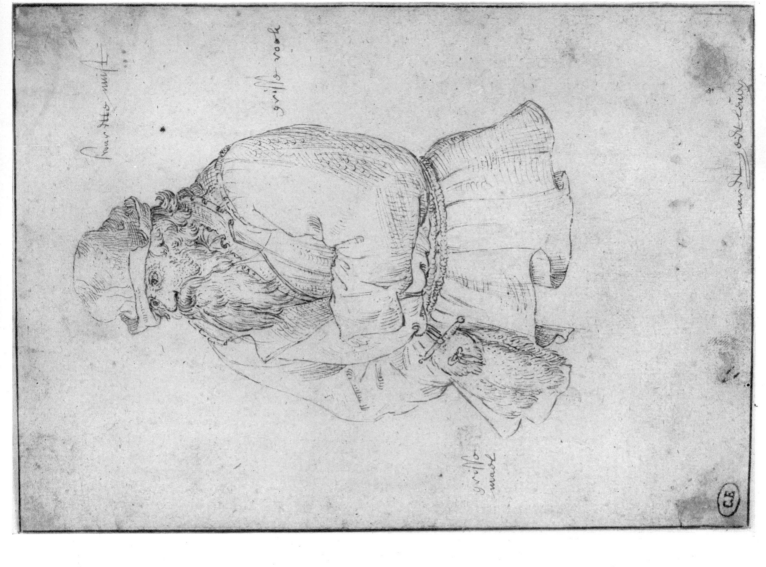

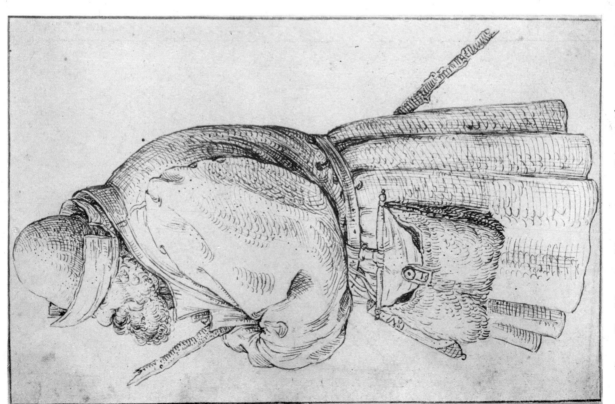

*III: Cat. No. 114. Half-Length Figure of a Peasant in Three-Quarter Profile, Looking to the Left. About 1564-65. Rotterdam, Boymans-van Beuningen Museum

*110: Cat. No. 113. Man with a Staff. About 1564. Frankfurt-am-Main, Städelsches Kunstinstitut

*112: Cat. No. 115. A Man Standing, Seen from the Back. About 1565.
Weimar, Schlossmuseum

*113: Cat. No. 116. Figure with a Tall Hat Seen from the Back; on the
Right a Second Figure Seen from the Back. After 1565.
Rotterdam, Boymans-van Beuningen Museum

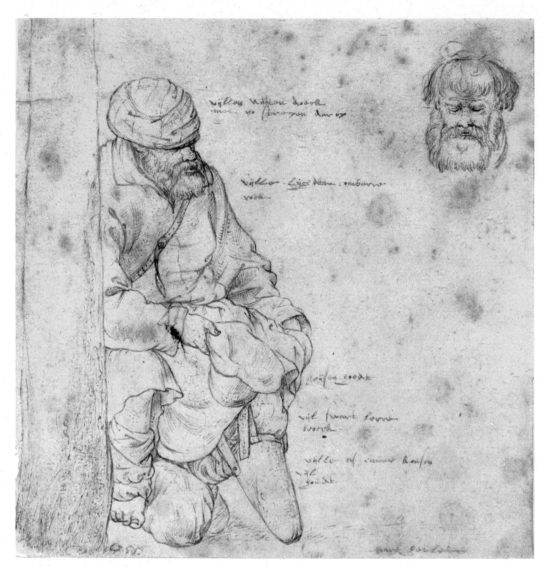

*114: Cat. No. 117. BEGGAR WITH A TURBAN, AND STUDY OF A HEAD. About 1565.
Amsterdam, Rijksmuseum

115: Cat. No. 118. Two Beggars Seated. About 1565. Berlin, Kupferstichkabinett

*116: Cat. No. 119. Seated Man seen from the Front, and Half-Length Figure Turned
Three Quarters to the Right. About or after 1565. Paris, F. Lugt Collection

*117: Cat. No. 120. Two Peasants in Half-Length. About or after 1565. Cleveland, Museum of Art, J. H. Wade Collection

*118: Cat. No. 121. SEATED PEASANT ASLEEP. About 1565. Dresden, Kupferstichkabinett

*119: Cat. No. 122. Two Seated Peasant Women Seen from the Back. About 1565. Dresden, Kupferstichkabinett

*120: Cat. No. 123. Peasant Woman, and Peasant Seen
from the Back, both in Half-Length. 1565 or later.
Amsterdam, Rijksmuseum

*121: Cat. No. 124. Peasant Woman Seen from the Back.
About 1565. Berlin, Kupferstichkabinett

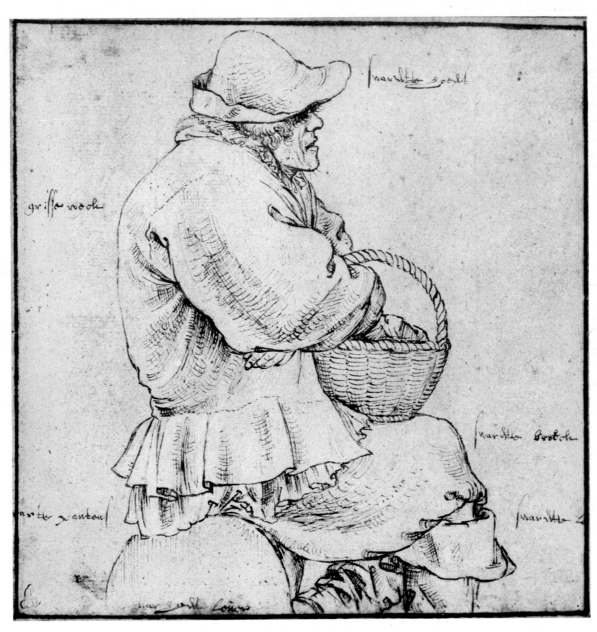

*122: Cat. No. 125. Seated Peasant, Seen in Profile, with Basket on his Lap.
About 1565 or later. Vienna, Albertina

123: Cat. No. 126. THE PAINTER AND THE CONNOISSEUR. About 1565 or later. Vienna, Albertina

III : COMPOSITIONS

124: Cat. No. 127. THE TEMPTATION OF ST. ANTHONY. Dated 1556. Oxford, Ashmolean Museum

125: Cat. No. 128. Big Fish Eat Little Fish. Dated 1556. Vienna, Albertina

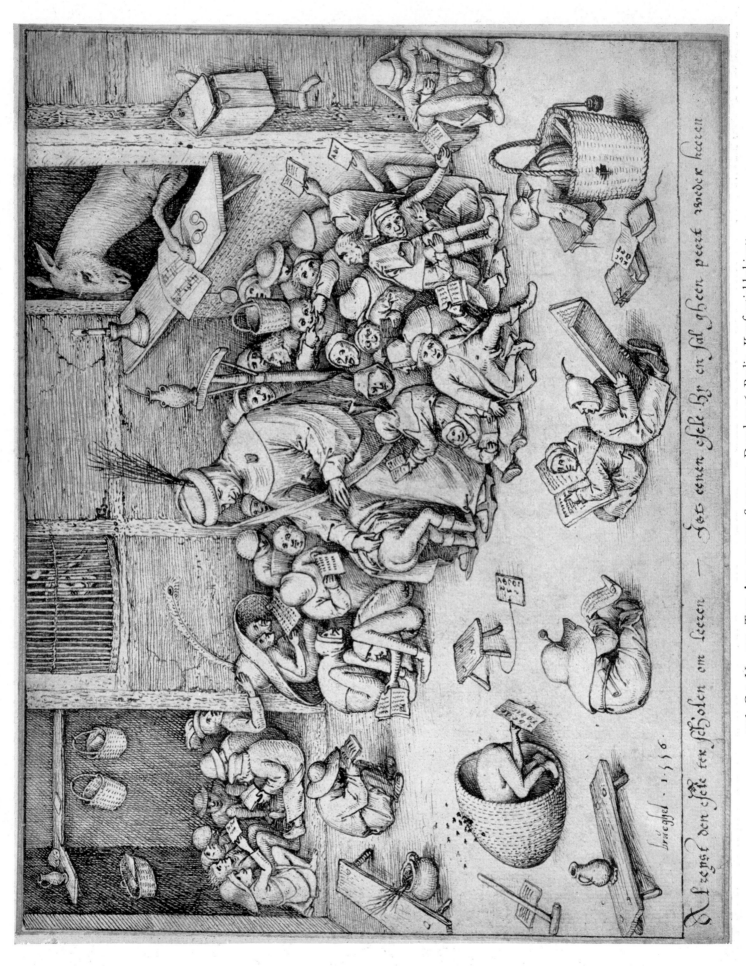

Bruegel · 1556.

By zynt den ezel ter schoolen om leeren — Ist eenen ezel. Br en sal gheen peert weder keeren

126: Cat. No. 129. THE ASS IN THE SCHOOL. Dated 1556. Berlin, Kupferstichkabinett

127: Cat. No. 130. AVARITIA. Dated 1556. London, British Museum

brueghel 1557

gula

128: Cat. No. 131. GULA. Dated 1557 Paris, F. Lugt Collection

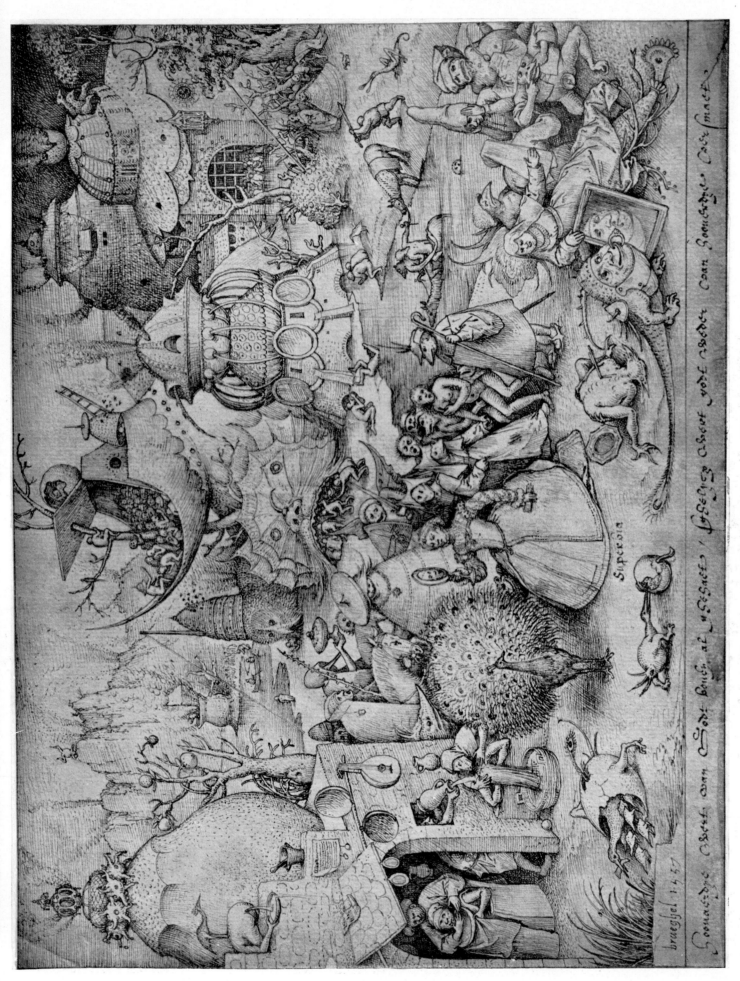

braeggel 1557

Superbia

Soouwighe Obbest oan Soot ban Obbist oe in Seenees / Goghes Obbest vol Asches / oan Soonsatige Cost moect

129: Cat. No. 132. SUPERBIA. Dated 1557. Paris, F. Lugt Collection

130 · Cat No 132 LUXURIA Dated 1557 Brussels Bibliothèque Royale

131: Cat. No. 134. IRA. Dated 1557. Florence, Uffizi

132: Cat. No. 135. INVIDIA. Dated 1557. Basle, Baron R. von Hirsch Collection

133: Cat. No. 136. Desidia. Dated 1557. Vienna, Albertina

134: Cat. No. 137. THE LAST JUDGEMENT. Dated 1558. Vienna, Albertina

137: Cat. No. 140. Skating Outside St. George's Gate. Dated 1559. Private Collection in America

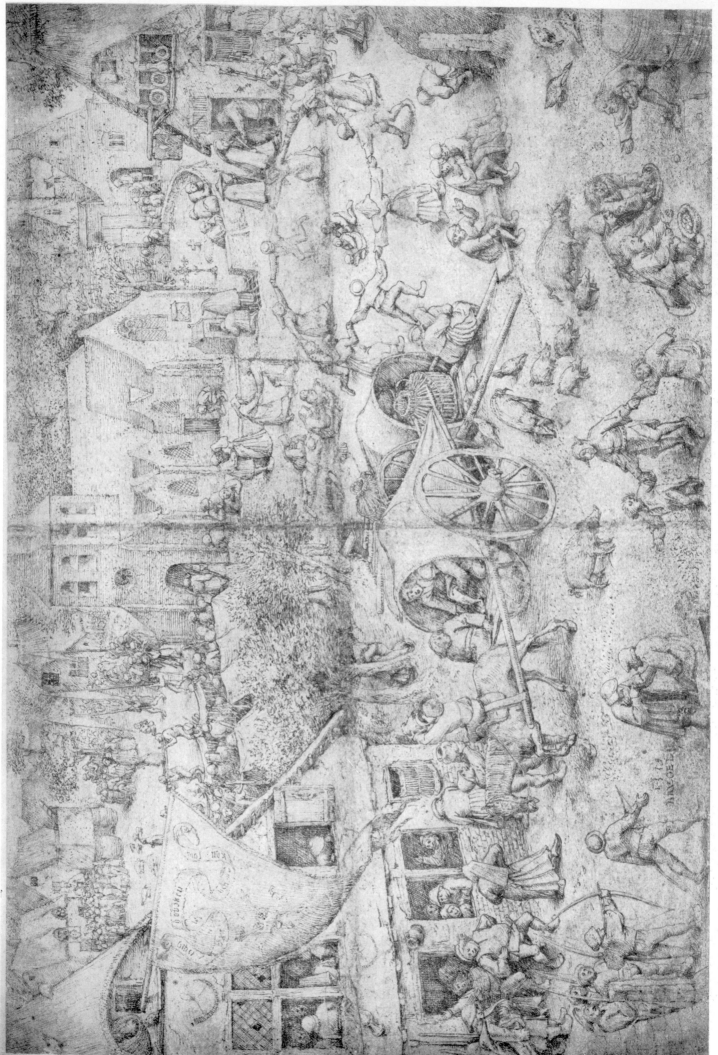

138: Cat. No. 141. The Kermess of Hoboken. Dated 1559. Formerly London, Oppenheimer Collection

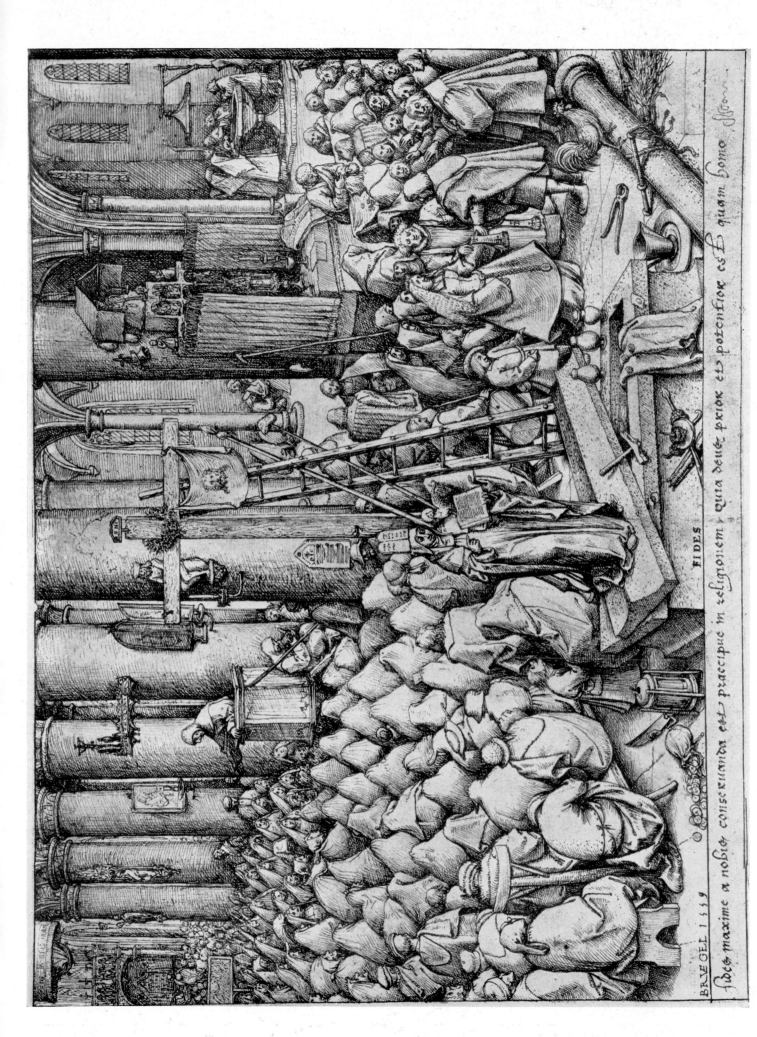

139: Cat. No. 142. FIDES. Dated 1559. Amsterdam, Rijksmuseum

140: Cat. No. 143. Charitas. Dated 1559. Rotterdam, Boymans-van Beuningen Museum

PRVDENCIA

BRVEGHEL 1559

Si prudens esse cupis in futurum prospectum ostende et quae possunt contingere animo tuo cuncta propone

141: Cat. No. 144. PRUDENTIA. Dated 1559. Brussels, Musées Royaux des Beaux-Arts

Iucundissima est Spei persuasio et vitæ imprimis. Necessaria inter tot aerumnas penecz intolerabilis.

BREGEL

142: Cat. No. 145. SPES. Dated 1559. Berlin, Kupferstichkabinett

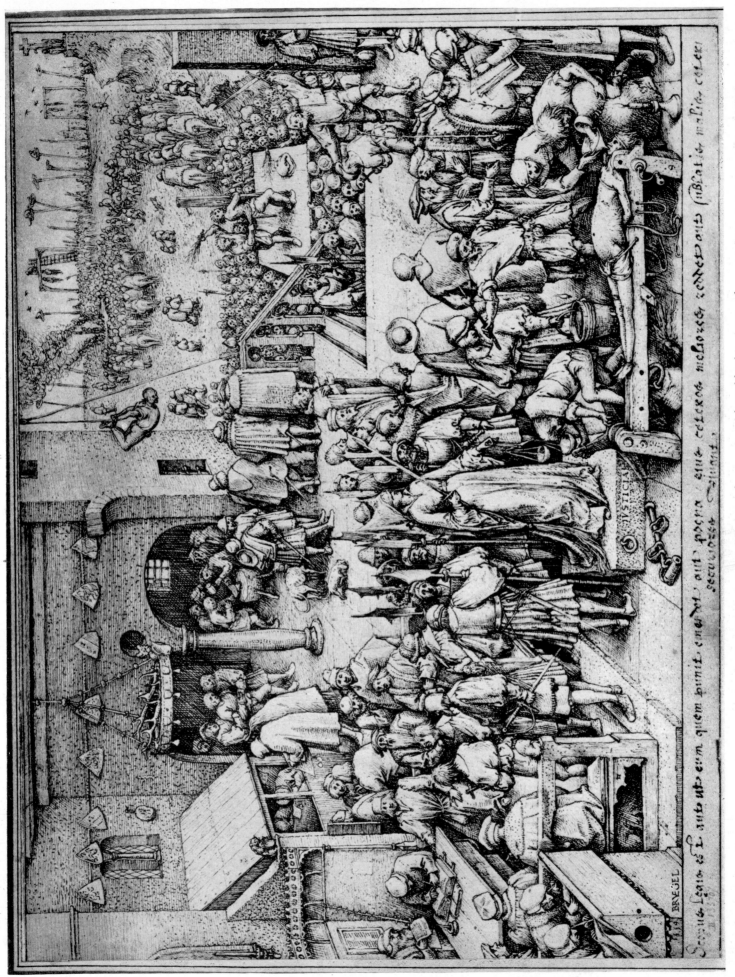

143: Cat. No. 146. JUSTITIA. Dated 1559. Brussels, Bibliothèque Royale

144: Cat. No. 147. FORTITUDO. Dated 1560. Rotterdam, Boymans-van Beuningen Museum

145: Cat. No. 148. Temperantia. Dateċ 1560. Rotterdam, Beymans-van Beuningen Museum

147: Cat. No. 150. THE FALL OF THE MAGICIAN. Dated 1544 (in error for 1564). Amsterdam, Rijksmuseum

148: Cat. No. 151. SPRING. Dated 1565. Vienna, Albertina.

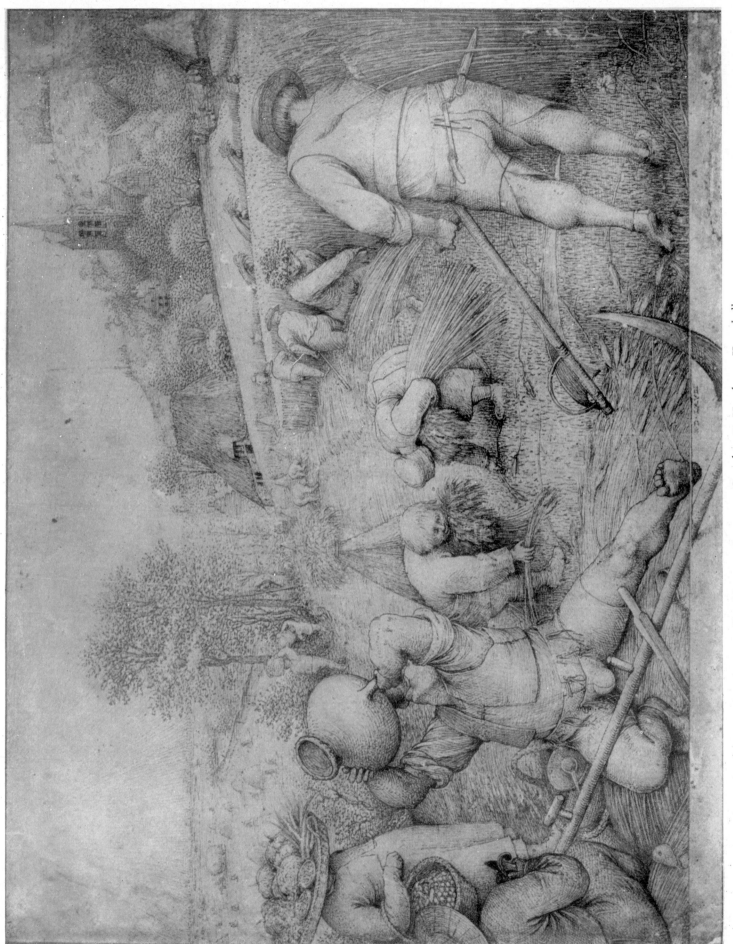

149: Cat. No. 152. SUMMER. Dated 1568. Hamburg, Kunsthalle

150: Cat. No. 153. The Marriage of Mopsus and Nisa. About or after 1566. New York, Metropolitan Museum of Art

151: Cat. No. 154. THE BEE-KEEPERS. About 1568. Berlin, Kupferstichkabinett

152: THE ALCHEMIST. Detail from Plate 136

COPIES AND ATTRIBUTIONS

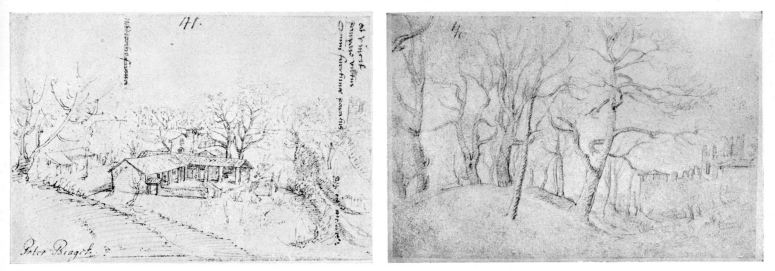

153–154: Cat. No. A1–A2. Pieter Bruegel (?): Italian Monastery; Wooded Landscape with a Castle on the Right.

155: Cat. No. A3. River Landscape. Etching

156: Cat. No. A4. Anonymus Fabriczy: VIEW OF VIENNE. Berlin, Kupfestichkabinett

157: Cat. No. A5. Anonymus Fabriczy: HILLY LANDSCAPE. (Verso of Plate 156.) Berlin, Kupferstichkabinett

158: Cat. No. A6. Anonymus Fabriczy (?): VIEW OF FONDI. Private Collection in America

159: Cat. No. A7. Anonymus Fabriczy (?): MOUNTAIN RANGE. The Hague, Bredius Museum

160: Cat. No. A8. Jacques Savery: Landscape with a Castle on Rocks. Princeton, N.J., Private Collection

161: Cat. No. A10. Jacques Savery: River Landscape with Distant View. Antwerp, Musée Plantin-Moretus

162: Cat. No. A11. Jacques Savery (?): Ruined Tower. Paris, F. Lugt Collection

163: Cat. No. A12. Jacques Savery (?): Landscape with Church and Tower in the Distance. Rotterdam, Boymans-van Beuningen Museum

164: Cat. No. A13. Jacques Savery (?): Village Landscape. Berlin, Kupferstichkabinett

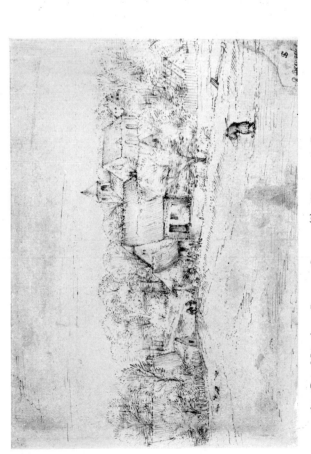

165: Cat. No. A15. Jacques Savery (?): Landscape with a Herd of Cattle. Amsterdam, Rijksmuseum

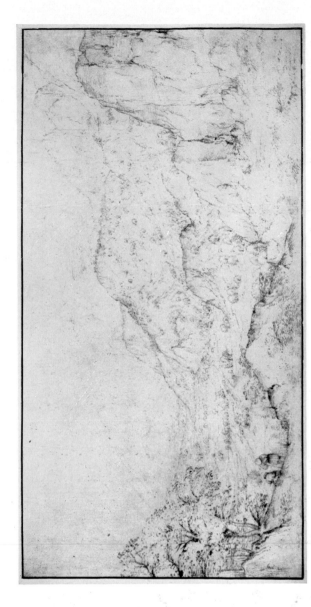

166: Cat. No. A14: Jacques Savery (?): Village Landscape with View of a Church. Amsterdam, Rijksmuseum

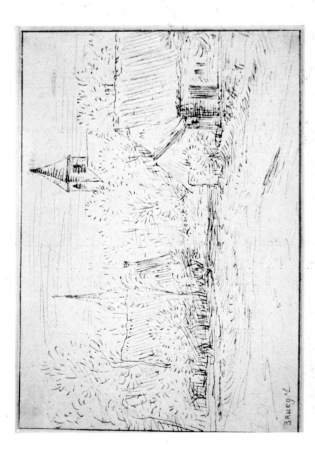

167: Cat. No. A16. Roeland Savery (?): Landscape with the Martinswand near Innsbruck. Berlin, Kupferstichkabinett

168: Cat. No. A17. Georg Hoefnagel: The Martinswand near Zirl. Vienna, Kunsthistorisches Museum·

169: Cat. No. A18. Roeland Savery (?): Landscape
Leiden, Prentenkabinet

170: Cat. No. A19. Roeland Savery (?): Landscape with a Brook.
Paris, F. Lugt Collection

171: Cat. No. A20. Roeland Savery: THE DREDGER. Chatsworth, Devonshire Collection

172: Cat. No. A21. Jan Brueghel the Elder (?): HILLSIDE WITH A VILLAGE ON THE RIGHT. Paris, Louvre

173: Cat. No. A22. Jan Brueghel the Elder (?): MOUNTAIN LANDSCAPE. Brunswick, Landesmuseum

174: Cat. No. A23. Jan Brueghel the Elder: LANDSCAPE WITH THE ROAD TO EMMAUS.
Rotterdam, Boymans-van Beuningen Museum

175: Cat. No. A24. Jan Brueghel the Elder (?): THE RIPA GRANDE IN ROME.
Chatsworth, Devonshire Collection

176: Cat. No. A25. Jan Brueghel the Elder: TRIUMPHAL ARCH. Chatsworth, Devonshire Collection

177: Cat. No. A26. Jan Brueghel the Elder: BASRODE. Berlin, Kupferstichkabinett

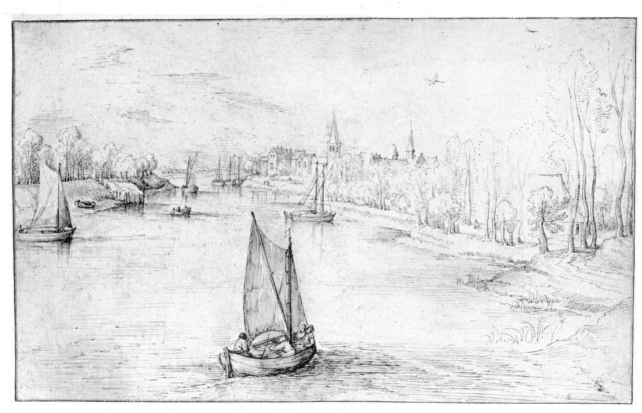

178: Cat. No. A27. Jan Brueghel the Elder: BASRODE. London, British Museum

179: Cat. No. A28. Jan Brueghel the Elder (?): FOREST LANDSCAPE WITH BEARS. London, British Museum

180: Cat. No A29. Jan Brueghel the Elder: THE ANGLER. Brussels, Musées Royaux

181: Cat. No. A32. Jan Brueghel the Elder (?): ALPINE LANDSCAPE WITH FOREST. Paris, F. Lugt Collection

182: Cat. No. A30. Jan Brueghel the Elder: ALPINE LANDSCAPE WITH PINE FOREST.
Rotterdam, Boymans-van Beuningen Museum

183: Cat. No. A33. Jan Brueghel the Elder (?): HUT WITH FENCE.
Munich, Graphische Sammlungen

184: Cat. No. A34. Jan Brueghel the Elder (?): BARN.
(Verso of Plate 183). Munich, Graphische Sammlungen

185: Cat. No. A31. Jan Brueghel the Elder: ALPINE LANDSCAPE WITH PINE FOREST.
Munich, Graphische Sammlungen

186: Cat. No. A35. Jan Brueghel the Elder: TOWN WITH BRIDGE.
Basle, Baron R. von Hirsch Collection

187: Cat. No. A36. Master of 1572 (?): ROCKY ISLAND.
Milan, Ambrosiana

188: Cat. No. A37. Pieter Brueghel the Younger (?):
MAN POURING OUT WATER. Paris, Louvre

189: Cat. No. A38. Copy after Pieter Bruegel the Elder (?): THREE MEN
IN CONVERSATION. Göttingen, Universitätsbibliothek

190: Cat. No. A39. Pieter Brueghel the Younger (?): THREE PEASANTS.
Ghent, Delacre Collection

191: Cat. No. A40. Pieter Brueghel
the Younger (?): A MASKED MAN.
Berlin, Kupferstichkabinett

192: Cat. No. A41. Pieter Brueghel the Younger: MAN WALKING; BEHIND HIM A WOMAN WITH A CHILD IN HER ARMS. Ghent, Delacre Collection

193: Cat. No. A43. Pieter Brueghel the Younger: BRAWLING PEASANTS.

194: Cat. No. A42. Pieter Brueghel the Younger: PEASANT WOMAN LEADING A DRUNKEN MAN HOME. Frankfurt-am-Main, Städelsches Kunstinstitut

195: Cat. No. A44. Pieter Brueghel the Younger: VILLAGE SCENE. Engraving after the painting in the Grisar Collection, Antwerp

196: Cat. No. A45. Jacques Savery: Formerly Berne, Dr. Eberhard Kornfeld Collection

197: Cat. No. A47. Georg Hoefnagel: Vienna, Christian Nebehay

198: Cat. No. A46. London, Vincent Korda Collection

199: Cat. No. A48. London, British Museum

THE PAINTER AND THE CONNOISSEUR. Copies after the original by Pieter Bruegel, Plate 123

200: Cat. No. A49. Pieter Brueghel the Younger: Dancers at a Village Wedding. London, British Museum

201: Cat. No. A50. Pieter Brueghel the Younger:
Group of Men and Women.
Budapest, National Gallery

202: Cat. No. A51. Pieter Brueghel the Younger:
Sheet of Studies
Besançon, Musée des Beaux-Arts

203: Cat. No. A55. Copy after Pieter Bruegel: THE EPILEPTIC WOMAN OF MEULEBEECK. Vienna, Albertina

204: Cat. No. A57. A. van Dyck after Bruegel: STUDY FOR THE FEAST OF ST. MARTIN

205: Pieter Balten: THE FEAST OF ST. MARTIN. Detail. Antwerp, Museum

CATALOGUE
OF THE DRAWINGS

LITERATURE QUOTED IN ABBREVIATED FORM

BASTELAER (oder B.): René van Bastelaer et Georges Hulin de Loo, *Pieter Bruegel l'Ancien, son œuvre et son temps*. Brussels, 1905–1907.

BASTELAER, ESTAMPES: René van Bastelaer, *Les Estampes de Pieter Bruegel l'Ancien*. Brussels, 1908.

BALDASS: Ludwig von Baldass, *Die niederländische Landschaftsmalerei von Patinier bis Bruegel. Jahrbuch der Kunsthistorischen Sammlungen des Allerhöchsten Kaiserhauses*, Jahrg. XXXIV, Vienna, 1918.

BENESCH, ALBERTINA KATALOG: Otto Benesch, *Die Zeichnungen der Niederländischen Schulen des XV. und XVI. Jahrhunderts. Beschreibender Katalog der Albertina*, vol. VII, Vienna, 1928.

BENESCH, NORTHERN RENAISSANCE: Otto Benesch, *The Art of the Renaissance in Northern Europe*. Cambridge, Mass., 1945.

BENESCH, KUNSTCHRONIK: Otto Benesch, *Charles de Tolnay, Die Zeichnungen Pieter Bruegels*. In: *Kunstchronik*, 6.Jahr , Heft 3, März 1953.

EBBINGE WUBBEN: J. C. Ebbinge Wubben, *De van Eyck à Bruegel. Catalogue Bibliothèque Nationale*. Paris, 1949.

FRIEDLÄNDER: M. J. Friedländer, *Pieter Bruegel*. Berlin, 1921.

BOCK-ROSENBERG, Berlin Catalogue: *Staatliche Museen zu Berlin. "Die Niederländischen Meister": Beschreibendes Verzeichnis der Zeichnungen von E. Bock und J. Rosenberg*. Frankfurt a/M., 1931 (Berlin, 1930). 2 vols.

G.D.B.A.: *Gazette des Beaux-Arts*, Paris.

HAUSENSTEIN: Wilhelm Hausenstein, *Der Bauern-Bruegel*, 1st edition, Munich, 1910; 2nd edition, Munich, 1920.

HOLLSTEIN: F. W. H. Hollstein, *Dutch and Flemish Etchings, Engravings and Woodcuts*, ca. 1450–1700. Vol. III, Amsterdam, n.d. (1950.)

HYMANS: Henry Hymans, *Pierre Bruegel le Vieux*, in: *Gazette des Beaux-Arts*. 1890, I; 1891, IV. u.V.

J.D.A.K.: *Jahrbuch der Kunsthistorischen Sammlungen des Allerhöchsten Kaiserhauses* (Vienna Yearbook), Vienna.

J.D.K.S.: *Jahrbuch der Kunsthistorischen Sammlungen in Wien, Neue Folge*.

J.D.PR.K.: *Jahrbuch der Preussischen Kunstsammlungen, Berlin* (Prussian Yearbook).

MICHEL: Edouard Michel, *Bruegel*. Paris, 1931.

POPHAM, CAT. BRITISH MUSEUM: *Catalogue of Drawings by Dutch and Flemish Artists in the British Museum*, vol. V. London, 1932.

ROMDAHL: Axel L. Romdahl, *Pieter Bruegel der Ältere und sein Kunstschaffen*. In: *Jahrbuch der Kunsthistorischen Sammlungen des Allerhöchsten Kaiserhauses*, XXV. Wien, 1905, Heft 3, S. 85 ff.

SEILERN: Antoine Seilern, *Flemish Paintings and Drawings at 56, Princes' Gate, London*. Vol. I, London, 1955.

STOCKHOLM CATALOGUE: *Catalogue of Dutch and Flemish Drawings*. Stockholm, 1953.

TOLNAY I: K. Tolnay, *Die Zeichnungen Pieter Bruegels*. Munich, 1925.

TOLNAY II: Charles de Tolnay, *The Drawings of Pieter Bruegel the Elder*. London, 1952. (A German edition was published in the same year in Zurich.)

VANBESELAERE: Walter Vanbeselaere, *Pieter Bruegel en het nederlandsche manierisme*. Tielt n.d. (1944).

CATALOGUE

LANDSCAPES

1 : Plate 1

RIVER VALLEY, WITH MOUNTAIN IN BACKGROUND. Paris, Louvre.

Pen and brown ink, on greyish-blue paper, in parts not well preserved. 175×265 mm. Dated below in centre, *1552*. False signature at upper right, *Bruegel fecit*. Damages in the paper near the middle of the sky.

It seems to me that this drawing – on account of its hesitant line – must be earlier than the *Mountain Landscape with Italian-style Cloister* (our No. 2), which dates from the same year. With the stress laid on the darker foreground with its broken lines, rather than on the distance, this drawing fore-shadows many elements found in Bruegel's later landscape style.

Lit.: *Bastelaer* No. 1; *Michel*, p. 91, pl. 63; *Tolnay II*, No. 3.

2 : Plate 2

MOUNTAIN LANDSCAPE WITH ITALIAN-STYLE CLOISTER. Berlin, Kupferstichkabinett.

Pen and brown ink, on white paper, partially coloured with water-colours. 186×328 mm. Signed and dated at lower left corner, *brueghel 1552*.

Tolnay rightly points out that the wide panoramic format has Netherlandish precedents. As the only surviving water-colour by Bruegel this sheet is of particular importance. The sky is a delicate blue, the hills on the distant horizon are bluish green and those in front are green, the houses are brown and some of the roofs brick-red. The foreground is in tones of grey. The figures were originally lightly sketched in. The landscape was clearly completed in the studio, with the addition of the trees in the foreground. Closely related to the present drawing in style is one first published by Wescher, from a small sketch-book, the definite attribution of which to Bruegel is fraught with difficulties. It is here reproduced among the attributions (our No. A1).

Lit.: *Bastelaer* No. 2; *Baldass*, *J.d.A.K.* XXXIV, 1918, p. 147; *Friedländer*, p. 38; *Michel*, p. 91, pl. 62; *Bock-Rosenberg, Berlin Catalogue*, No. 5537, pl. 18; P. Wescher, *Pantheon*, Jahrgang IV, April 1931, No. 4, Bericht-Beilage, p. XXV, repr. p. 182; *Tolnay II*, No. 2.

3 : Plate 3

LANDSCAPE WITH WALLED TOWN. London, British Museum.

Pen and brown ink in several tones. Crease in the centre.

237×335 mm. Signed and dated in lower right corner, *p brueghel 1553*. Traces of a watermark.

The beginnings of the new influence of Campagnola can clearly be seen in this broadly visualized landscape with its troubled, cloudy sky. Tolnay believes that this landscape can be identified as the first of an early landscape series. With the castle in the centre of the walled town this sheet is obviously a composed landscape. There is much in favour of the theory that it was executed during the return journey to the Nether-lands, while the artist was still in Italy.

Lit.: Popham, *Drawings of the early Flemish School*, London, 1926, pl. 67; *Michel*, p. 92, pl. 66; Popham, *Catalogue of the Drawings by Dutch and Flemish Artists in the British Museum*, V, 1932, p. 142, No. 1; Benesch, *Northern Renaissance*, p. 93; *Tolnay II*, No. 7.

4 : Plate 4

LANDSCAPE WITH RIVER AND MOUNTAINS. London, British Museum.

Pen and ink in several tones of brown, on white paper. 228×338 mm. Dated at lower left corner, *1553*. Watermark, circle with coat of arms.

Hymans was the first to recognize the London drawing as Bruegel's original, in opposition to Bastelaer, who tried to see the original in the copy at the Louvre. In the use made of the planes of the foreground, and even more in the figures moving into the landscape, this composite landscape drawing shows the increasing influence of Campagnola.

Lit.: Hymans, *G.d.B.A.*, 1890, I, p. 367; *Bastelaer*, No. 17; *Michel*, p. 93, pl. 67; Popham, *Catalogue of Drawings by Dutch and Flemish Artists in the British Museum*, V, 1932, p. 142, No. 2; Baldass, *J.d.A.K.*, XXXIV, No. 4, pp. 17 ff. (the Paris copy); *Tolnay II*, No. 8.

5 : Plate 5

ALPINE LANDSCAPE. Paris, Louvre.

Pen and brown ink in several tones, on white, foxed paper. 236×343 mm. Dated at centre of lower margin, *1553*. Tolnay does not consider the signature, BRVEGHEL, to be genuine. Collector's mark; Mariette.

This landscape, with the great mountains flanking it in the foreground, marks a new step in Bruegel's assimilation of Venetian landscape art. Already referred to in Mariette's *Abecedario*, this sheet belongs to the series of Bruegel's grandiose landscape compositions displaying all the natural wildness of mountains. Tolnay believes that this drawing is a completely free composition executed in the studio, but the free and forceful rendering of the shadows, in contrast, for example, to the *Landscape with River and Mountains* (our No. 4), points to it having been drawn to a great extent from nature. In the etching, first published by Hollstein, after a drawing by Bruegel in the Print Room at Amsterdam, there is a similar deep mountain valley, surrounded by crags.

Lit.: *Friedländer*, p. 42; *Michel*, p. 93 and pl. 68; *Vanbeselaere*, p. 34, pl. 6; *Ebbinge Wubben*, No. 45; Mariette, *Archives de l'art français*, 1851–1853, p. 188; *Tolnay II*, No. 10; *Hollstein III*, p. 255, No. 2a.

6 : Plate 6

LANDSCAPE WITH ROCKY MOUNTAINS. Dresden, Kupferstichkabinett.

Pen and brown ink in several tones, on white paper. 175× 303 mm. Cut at the margins. About 1553.

Tolnay was the first to recognize this drawing as a landscape by Bruegel. Woermann had erroneously placed it among the Italian drawings as the work of Domenichino. Tolnay also thinks that the motif of the lofty mountain on the left recurs in the large landscape etching of the *Magdalena Poenitens* (Bastelaer, *Estampes*, No. 8), but it seems to me that this mountain formation has a closer relationship with the background of the large *Solicitudo rustica* (Bastelaer, *Estampes*, No. 12). The drawing itself is probably a sketch executed from nature.

Lit.: Woermann, *Handzeichnungen alter Meister in Dresden*, Mappe VI, pl. 23, No. 219; *Tolnay II*, No. 13.

7 : Plate 7

RIVER VALLEY. Dresden, Kupferstichkabinett.

Pen and brown ink in several tones, on white paper. 134× 323 mm. About 1553–54.

This large, panorama-like distant view reveals a masterly development of the freedom of style found in the landscape, *River Valley, with Mountain in Background* (our No. 1), of 1552. It would seem that, with the exception of the indications of the flanking rocks in the right foreground, we have here a sheet drawn from nature. Tolnay mentions the suggestion made by Dr. E. Bier that this is a view of the Ticino Valley with the two castles, Castello Grande (Uri) and Castello Montebello (Schwyz), from the Italian side, in which case it must have been drawn during Bruegel's return journey from Italy in 1553–54. Portions of this landscape were used again by Bruegel on several occasions. Romdahl already noted its use in the background of the landscape *Insidiosus Auceps* (Bastelaer, *Estampes*, No. 10). Tolnay considers that the mountains on the left were the basis for the much steeper rocks in the right background of the *Magdalena Poenitens*.

Lit.: Woermann, *Handzeichnungen alter Meister in Dresden*, Mappe IV, pl. 13, No. 130; *Romdahl*, pp. 153–54; *Bastelaer*, No. 3; *Michel*, pl. 69; *Tolnay II*, No. 18.

8 : Plate 8

ALPINE RANGE. Dresden, Kupferstichkabinett.

Pen and brown ink in several tones, on white paper. 106× 324 mm. About 1553–54.

This drawing is a typical example of a rapid, free sketch from nature.

Lit.: Woermann, *op. cit.*; Mappe IV, pl. 13, No. 131; *Bastelaer*, No. 4; *Tolnay II*, No. 11.

9 : Plate 9

LANDSCAPE WITH RIVER VALLEY AND MOUNTAINS OF MEDIUM HEIGHT. Chatsworth, Devonshire Collection.

Pen and brown ink in several tones, on white paper. 133× 287 mm.

Tolnay, whose attention was drawn to this sketch by Dr. Erhard Göpel, of Leipzig, was the first to publish it as by Bruegel. Unfortunately this masterly sheet suffered severe damage as a result of the war, and it is here reproduced from an old photograph taken before its partial destruction.

Lit.: *Tolnay II*, No. 12.

10 : Plate 10

GIGANTIC MOUNTAINS. Dresden, Kupferstichkabinett.

Pen and brown ink in several tones, on white paper. 124× 185 mm. The signature at the lower right corner is not authentic.

Lit.: *Bastelaer*, No. 5; *Michel*, pl. 70; *Tolnay II*, No. 15.

11 : Plate 11

LANDSCAPE WITH RANGE OF MOUNTAINS. Chatsworth, Devonshire Collection.

Pen and brown ink in several tones, on white paper. 175× 256 mm.

Probably drawn from nature, this study is also reproduced from an old photograph, because, like No. 9, it was severely damaged during the war. The steep summit, half hidden by mist, is found again, reversed, in the right background of *Paysage Alpestre* (Bastelaer, *Estampes*, No. 9).

Lit.: *Tolnay II*, No. 14.

12 : Plate 12

ALPINE LANDSCAPE. London, Count Antoine Seilern Collection.

Pen and brown ink in several tones, on white paper. 195× 322 mm. About 1555–56.

The masterly effect of this drawing rests on the manifold nuances of the strokes of the pen, by means of which light and shade are rendered in the most delicate manner. As is shown by the drawing of the right foreground, this large sheet must obviously have been finished, at the least, in the studio. Tolnay points out that the motif of the high crag on the right occurs again in a related, but much altered, form, in the large alpine landscape, *Paysage Alpestre* (Bastelaer, *Estampes*, No. 9). He also claims to see in the mountain range in the right background of the *Magdalena Poenitens* (Bastelaer, *Estampes*, No. 8) a reminiscence of the left half of the present drawing. But the two boulders in the water in the foreground of this drawing also appear again in the large mountain landscape (Bastelaer, *Estampes*, No. 9).

Lit.: A. E. Popham, *Vasari Society*, 2nd Series, XII, 1931, No. 10; A. E. Popham, *Fenwick Catalogue*, p. 179, pl. LXX; *Tolnay II*, No. 22; Seilern, *Catalogue*, No. 10.

13 : Plate 13

MOUNTAIN RAVINE. Paris, Louvre.

Pen and ink in several tones of brown, on grey-brown, yellowed paper. Very badly preserved. 290×430 mm. Remains of a signature (Br)*ueghel*, and parts of a barely legible, faded date (15)55.

This badly preserved sheet, with grey washes added later, particularly in the centre, is the only surviving preliminary drawing for an engraving of the large landscape series (Bastelaer, *Estampes*, No. 9). In the engraving itself changes were made, especially in the centre foreground. The two rocks in the centre foreground of the engraving, as well as the accessory figures, were obviously added at the engraving stage. These two rocks are very closely related to those in the water in the *Alpine Landscape* (our No. 12).

Lit.: *Bastelaer*, No. 20; *Michel*, pl. 71; *Tolnay II*, No. 23.

14 : Plate 14

ALPINE LANDSCAPE WITH AN ARTIST SKETCHING. London, Count Antoine Seilern Collection.

Pen and ink in several tones of brown, and some traces of preliminary drawing in black chalk. 277×396 mm. Inscribed in an old hand at the lower left corner, *de ouden Breugel*. About 1555–56?

Popham has rightly drawn attention to the relationship between this grandiose landscape composition and our No. 12. The figure of the artist sketching the landscape recurs frequently at this time. In Bruegel's own work it is found again in the Hufnagel engraving after his *Rape of Psyche* (Bastelaer, *Estampes*, No. 1). According to Tolnay the mountain path in the right background recurs, reversed, in the mountain landscape (Bastelaer, *Estampes*, No. 9), but I cannot agree with him.

Lit.: A. E. Popham, *Two Landscape Drawings by Pieter Bruegel the Elder*, The Burlington Magazine, XCI, 1949, pp. 319 ff.; *Tolnay II*, No. 21; Seilern, *Catalogue*, No. 9.

15 : Plate 15

ALPINE LANDSCAPE WITH TWO MULES. London, Count Antoine Seilern Collection.

Pen and brown ink in several tones, on white paper. 294× 425 mm. About 1555–56.

Count Seilern believes that this large landscape composition is slightly earlier than our No. 14. Tolnay's assertion that it is a little later is substantiated by the fact that the low rocks on the left, which – as Popham has pointed out – are found again in the engraving *Insidiosus Auceps* (Bastelaer, *Estampes*, No. 10), can also be seen in the *Landscape with Range of Mountains* (our No. 16), which is dated, rather illegibly near the centre of the lower margin, 1556. The lofty pines on the right are related to the landscape of the *Magdalena Poenitens*. The dark mountain massif slightly to the right of the centre, though seen from the other side, reminds one of the similar mountain formation on the drawing *Gigantic Mountains* (our No. 10).

Lit.: A. E. Popham, *Two Landscape Drawings by Pieter Bruegel the Elder*, The Burlington Magazine, XCI, 1949, pp. 319 ff.; *Tolnay II*, No. 20; Seilern, *Catalogue*, No. 8.

16 : Plate 16

LANDSCAPE WITH RANGE OF MOUNTAINS. (*Recto* of No. 17.) Chatsworth, Devonshire Collection.

Pen and ink in several tones of brown, on white paper. 237×360 mm. Signed and dated, rather illegibly, to right of centre of lower margin, *bruegel 1556*. (The Keeper of the Chatsworth Collections, Mr. T. Wragg, has, independently of myself, also read the date as *1556*.)

I do not consider Tolnay's doubts about the signature to be justified. This drawing, which Tolnay was the first to publish, was severely damaged by water during the war, and is reproduced here from an old photograph. The rocks on the left are the same as those on the *Insidiosus Auceps* (Bastelaer, *Estampes*, No. 10). The dating of this sheet makes it possible to date this whole group of drawings to about 1556. Tolnay believes that this landscape, like that on the drawing *River Valley* (our No. 7), also shows part of the Ticino Valley. The fact that the back of the drawing has been rubbed over with red chalk shows that the sheet was originally intended for reproduction.

Lit.: *Tolnay II*, No. 19.

Fig. 1   Cat. No. 17

17 : Fig. 1

SKETCH OF A GROUP OF ROCKS. (*Verso* of No. 16.) Chatsworth, Devonshire Collection.

About 1555–56.

On the back of the *Landscape with Range of Mountains* (our No. 16), close to the right margin, is a slight sketch of a group of rocks, which hitherto has been overlooked.

18 : Plate 17

ALPINE LANDSCAPE. Cambridge, Mass., Fogg Art Museum (formerly Charles Loeser Collection).

Pen and brown ink in several tones, on white paper. Not well preserved. Partially restored with light brown watercolours. 305×456 mm. About 1556.

It seems to me that Tolnay, who first published it, has dated this obviously composite large mountain landscape a little too early (1554–55). In my opinion it is related to the large landscape engravings of about 1556. I have to thank Miss Agnes Mongan, of the Fogg Art Museum, Cambridge, Mass., for the following report on the state of preservation of this drawing: 'The drawing is pasted to a heavy paper which seems to be at least of eighteenth century origin. At some time this heavy paper was folded down the centre, and the crease shows distinctly. When the drawing was pasted to the backing a poor adhesive was used which left air pockets which were later ironed down. The adhesive has stained the drawing at the right, across the bottom and at the left, and the ironing has given it a smooth surface, in fact a shiny appearance which is not very pleasant, although this can be seen only when you look at the drawing out of its frame and in a raking light. The drawing has been mended, as you can see even in the reproduction, at the lower left, and at the right centre foreground. Also there is a poorly mended tear which runs in an arc from the base of the steeple to the front left foreground'. The drawing is surrounded by a dark line about one-sixteenth of an inch from the margin. The fact that the drawing continues beyond this line on both sides shows that it was originally larger.

Lit.: Sachs and Mongan, *Drawings in the Fogg Museum of Art*, No. 459, fig. 234; *Tolnay II*, No. 17.

19 : Plate 19

VIEW OF WALTERSSPURG. Brunswick, Maine, Bowdoin College Museum of Fine Arts.

Pen and brown ink in several tones, on white paper. 317× 263 mm. Inscribed at the top, perhaps in Bruegel's own hand, *Waltersspurg*. On the *verso*, in chalk, *Von . . . Brugel no. 56.* About 1553–54.

Dr. Rosenberg has observed that this drawing may have been cut both on the right and on the left; he believes that the format was originally the same as that of the drawing in the Fogg Art Museum (our No. 18), but the composition, especially that of the foreground, speaks against this

supposition. Benesch discusses the identification of the locality in connection with our No. 21.

Lit.: F. J. Mather, Jr., *Art in America*, II (1914), p. 108, fig 1; Benesch, *Kunstchronik*, 1953, p. 79; *Tolnay II*, No. 16.

20 : Plate 20

MOUNTAIN LANDSCAPE WITH FIR TREE AND A CROSS IN LEFT FOREGROUND. Rotterdam, Boymans-van Beuningen Museum (F. Koenigs Collection).

Pen, brown ink and wash, on reddish-white paper. 236×275 mm. About 1553–54.

Swarzenski and Schilling were the first to describe this sheet as a drawing by Bruegel. Tolnay rejects this attribution, but to me (as it did to Benesch and after him also to Grossmann) it seems that this is a much redrawn original, to which wash was later applied, and the effect of which has suffered as a result of the redrawing by a later hand.

Lit.: G. Swarzenski and E. Schilling, *Handzeichnungen alter Meister aus deutschem Privatbesitz*, Frankfurt a/M., 1924, No. 22; Benesch, *Kunstchronik*, 1953, p. 79; Grossmann, *The Drawings of Pieter Bruegel the Elder and some Problems of Attribution*, Boymans Museum Bulletin, Vol. V, No. 2, 3; *Tolnay II*, No. A8.

21 : Plate 18

THE LARGE RHINE LANDSCAPE. New York, Pierpont Morgan Library.

Pen and ink in several tones of brown, on white paper. 350×435 mm. Signed at lower right corner: P. BRVEGEL. About 1553–54.

In the way in which the freely-drawn foreground details combine with the whole landscape this large drawing is one of the most accomplished sheets by Bruegel. It originally came to light at an auction at Christie's. Benesch has identified the locality as Burg Jorgenberg and the village of Ruis.

Lit.: Catalogue of the Sale of 16th May, 1952, Christie's, London, Lot 41; Benesch, *Kunstchronik*, 1953, p. 79; Grossmann, *New Light on Bruegel*, *The Burlington Magazine*, CI, September/October 1959, p. 345.

22 : Plate 21

LANDSCAPE WITH TOWN AND ST. JEROME. Zürich, Dr. Felix Somary Collection (formerly Liechtenstein Collection).

Pen and brown ink in several tones, on white paper. 235× 338 mm. Dated at lower left corner (1)553.

This drawing is a free, rapidly sketched landscape composition, with a great tree in the foreground. In this respect it belongs to a group together with the doubtful sheet in Berlin (our No. 23) and the *Sea Landscape* (our No. 25), also in Berlin, dating from about 1559. In the composition of the section of the landscape with the town wall there are reminiscences of the *Landscape with walled Town* (our No. 3).

Regteren Altena's attribution of this drawing to Jan Brueghel the Elder seems to me wrong.

Lit.: Schönbrunner-Meder, *Handzeichnungen alter Meister aus der Albertina und anderen Sammlungen*, No. 1393; J. Q. van Regteren Altena, *Pieter of Jan Brueghel, Oude Jaarboek*, IV series, I, p. 107; *Tolnay II*, No. 9.

23 : Plate 24

LARGE LANDSCAPE WITH TREES AND A CHURCH. (*Recto* of No. 24.) Berlin, Kupferstichkabinett.

Pen and several tones of brown ink. 329×466 mm. Faded remains of a signature at lower left corner, *.ruegel*, and above it *1554*. There is some damage on the right of the crease.

This drawing was first published by F. Lugt as an original Bruegel inspired by one of Campagnola's landscapes, but Tolnay in 1929 disputed this, and maintained that the so-called Campagnola model is an Italian copy based on the Bruegel drawing. Tolnay also doubts, like Regteren Altena, whether this sheet is an original drawing by Bruegel. In fact, compared with other drawings rich in detail, this one shows many shortcomings, but I am in no way sure that it is, as Regteren Altena supposes, a copy by Jan Brueghel. In any case the drawing is so important as a landscape composition, that it is reproduced here among the originals. Lugt has rightly drawn attention to the *verso*, which is here reproduced for the first time (No. 24). We know so little about the style of the initial sketches of Bruegel's landscape compositions, that, even if the authenticity of this sheet is in doubt, it is essential for purposes of study. In certain decisive elements – compare the way in which the horsemen are sketched – it seems to me to be related to Bruegel's *Landscape with River and Mountains* (our No. 4). In the context of the reproductions in this volume, both sides of this sheet belong to the rapid, grandiose landscape compositions of the late fifties.

Lit.: *Bastelaer*, No. 21; F. Lugt, *Pieter Bruegel und Italien*, in *Festschrift für M. J. Friedländer*, Leipzig, 1927, pp. 116 ff.; Tolnay, *Beiträge zu Bruegels Zeichnungen, J.d.pr.K.*, L, Berlin, 1929, p. 196; Bock-Rosenberg, *Berlin Catalogue*, No. 1202; J. Q. van Regteren Altena, *op. cit.*; F. Lugt, *Beiträge zu dem Katalog der Niederländischen Handzeichnungen in Berlin, J.d.pr. K.*, LII, Berlin, 1931, p. 38; *Tolnay II*, No. A6.

24 : Plate 23

LANDSCAPE WITH TWO HORSEMEN. (*Verso* of No. 23). Berlin, Kupferstichkabinett.

329×466 mm. About 1554? See No. 23.

25 : Plate 22

SEA LANDSCAPE WITH ROCKY ISLAND AND AN ITALIAN-STYLE CLOISTER; WITH THE HOLY FAMILY IN THE FOREGROUND. Berlin, Kupferstichkabinett.

Pen and brown ink, in several tones graduated for the different levels, in the foreground brownish violet. 203×282

mm. Signed at the lower right corner, *bruegel f.* On the *verso* strokes with the pen. About or after 1559.

While Friedländer, Baldass, Gustav Glück and Seilern rightly date this landscape to around or after 1559, Tolnay includes it among the earlier works. The present drawing is a fundamental example of the composite landscape, which, though less exact in detail and boldly executed in rather rapid strokes, is related in style to the large landscape etchings of after 1555.

Lit.: *Bastelaer*, No. 22; *Friedländer*, p. 160; Baldass, *op. cit.*; Gustav Glück, *Bruegels Gemälde*, Vienna, 1932 and 1951; Bock-Rosenberg, *Berlin Catalogue*, No. 5730; *Tolnay II*, No. 6.

26 : Plate 25

VISTA OF REGGIO. Rotterdam, Boymans-van Beuningen Museum (formerly F. Koenigs Collection).

Pen and ink, in warm tones of bistre, on slightly reddish paper. The grey and brown washes added later. 153×241 mm. Collector's mark, *FK*. Inscribed on the *verso* in an old hand, *Claude Lorrain . . . 24 florin*, and above this, in pencil, *Claude Gelee dit le Lorrain r.Nr.9*. About or after 1559.

Tolnay thinks that this is the original study of Reggio made by Bruegel during his journey to Sicily in about 1552–53. But the present drawing is, as he admits, the preliminary study in reverse for the engraving *The Naval Battle in the Straits of Messina* (Bastelaer, *Estampes*, No. 96) and its style, with the confidence and far-reaching individuality of its line, surely points to its having been executed about or after 1559. In its present condition the drawing has not only been extensively altered by the wash, but has also been worked over by a later hand, especially in the left third and in the hills in the background. Perhaps influenced by the inscription on the back, Regteren Altena has attributed the wash and re-drawing to Claude Lorrain, though there is no compelling proof of this. Jan Brueghel the Elder often washed his drawings in a similar way, as is shown in the drawing by him reproduced in Swarzenski and Schilling.

Lit.: Swarzenski and Schilling, *op. cit.*, No. 33; *Tolnay II*, No. 5.

The Small Landscapes

27 : Plate 26

ROCKY LANDSCAPE WITH CASTLE AND RIVER VALLEY. Vienna, Akademie der bildenden Künste, Kupferstichkabinett.

Pen and brown and yellow ink, on white paper. 136×210 mm. Signed and dated at lower left corner, P BRVEGEL *1559*.

This drawing is the earliest of Bruegel's small landscapes. In Tolnay's reproduction the landscape has been cut on the right and at the bottom.

Lit.: *Bastelaer*, No. 23; *Tolnay II*, No. 25.

28 : Plate 27

MOUNTAINOUS LANDSCAPE WITH NARROW PATH BETWEEN ROCKS; AND RIVER VALLEY AT LEFT. Berlin, Kupferstichkabinett (formerly von Beckerath Collection).

Pen and yellowish ink, on white paper. 144×189 mm. Signed and dated at lower right corner, BRVEGEL *1560*. (Bastelaer and Friedländer both read the date wrongly as 1566.)

Lit.: *Bastelaer*, No. 30; *Friedländer*, p. 191; Bock-Rosenberg, *Berlin Catalogue*, No. 5764; *Michel*, pl. 73; *Tolnay II*, No. 30.

29 : Plate 28

RIVER LANDSCAPE WITH LARGE ROCKS AT LEFT, AND A SAILING-BOAT. Berlin, Kupferstichkabinett (formerly Suermondt Collection).

Pen and light-brown ink, on white paper. 143×190 mm. Signed and dated at lower margin, close to centre, P. BRVEGEL *1560*.

Lit.: *Bastelaer*, No. 24; *Friedländer*, p. 21; *Michel*, pl. 72; Bock-Rosenberg, *Berlin Catalogue*, No. 712, pl. 19; *Tolnay II*, No. 29.

30 : Plate 29

ROCKY RIVER LANDSCAPE. Amsterdam, Rijksmuseum (formerly Heseltine-Richter Collection).

Pen and light-yellowish ink, darker only in the left foreground, on yellowish-white paper. 144×190 mm. Signed and dated at lower right corner, P. BRVEGEL *1560*.

Lit.: *Catalogue of the Auction of the Heseltine-Richter Collection*, Amsterdam, Frederik Muller and Company, 27-28 May, 1913, lot 69, pl. 6; *Tolnay II*, No. 28.

31 : Plate 30

ROCKY LANDSCAPE. Paris, F. Lugt Collection.

Pen and yellowish-brown ink, on white paper. 108×201 mm. Signed and dated at lower left corner, P BRVEGEL *1560*. Watermark, fragment of a crown.

In the second edition of his book Tolnay withdrew his doubts about this drawing.

Lit.: *Tolnay II*, No. 27.

32 : Plate 31

ROCKY LANDSCAPE WITH A CASTLE. London, Count Antoine Seilern Collection.

Pen and yellowish ink, on white paper; slight traces of preliminary drawing in black chalk. 145×192 mm. Signed and dated in upper left corner, P. BRVEGEL *1560*.

Tolnay has withdrawn his doubts about the authenticity of this drawing. A certain freedom and looseness of line is often particularly characteristic of Bruegel's small landscape drawings.

Lit.: *Tolnay II*, No. 26; Seilern, *Catalogue*, No. 12.

33 : Plate 32

LANDSCAPE WITH CASTLE ON HILL TO THE RIGHT. Berlin, Kupferstichkabinett.

Pen and ink in several tones of brown, dark brown in the foreground. 144×193 mm. About 1560.

First published by Friedländer as a Bruegel drawing, this landscape was, in my opinion wrongly, rejected by Tolnay.

Lit.: *Bastelaer*, No. 31; *Friedländer*, p. 33, No. 16; Bock-Rosenberg, *Berlin Catalogue*, No. 717.

34 : Plate 33

VILLAGE LANDSCAPE WITH PEASANTS AND A TREE. London, Count Antoine Seilern Collection.

Pen and very light and darker brown ink, on white paper. 145×187 mm. Signed and dated at lower right corner, P. BRVEGEL *1560*.

This drawing was originally published by E. Michel, and was then in the collection of Dr. E. S. Aveyron, France.

Lit.: E. Michel, *Bruegel et la Critique moderne*, in *G.d.B.A.*, 1950, pp. 121 ff; *Tolnay II*, addenda No. 3.

35 : Plate 34

VILLAGE LANDSCAPE WITH PEASANT FAMILY IN THE FOREGROUND. Vienna, Akademie der bildenden Künste, Kupferstichkabinett.

Pen and very light and somewhat darker brown ink, on white paper. 140×185 mm. Signed and dated at lower right corner, BRVEGEL *1560*.

Lit.: *Bastelaer*, No. 13; *Tolnay II*, No. 32.

36 : Plate 35

LANDSCAPE WITH A VILLAGE AND A FAMILY WALKING IN THE FOREGROUND. Paris, Louvre.

Pen and yellowish ink, on white paper. 143×190 mm. Signed and dated at lower right corner, P BRVEGEL *1560*.

Like No. 35 this drawing belongs to the series of intimate, small homeland landscapes.

Lit.: *Bastelaer*, No. 12; *Michel*, pl. 75; *Tolnay II*, No. 33.

37 : Plate 36

VILLAGE LANDSCAPE WITH CHURCH IN THE FOREGROUND. Berlin, Kupferstichkabinett.

Pen and yellowish-brown ink, on white paper. 143×190 mm. Signed and dated at lower left corner, P BRVEGEL *1560*.

Like Nos. 35 and 36 this drawing belongs to the intimate, small homeland landscapes.

Lit.: *Bastelaer*, No. 14; *Friedländer*, p. 15; *Michel*, pl. 74; Bock-Rosenberg, *Berlin Catalogue*, No. 714; *Tolnay II*, No. 31.

38 : Plate 37

CASTLE WITH ROUND TOWERS; AT THE LEFT A RIVER. Berlin, Kupferstichkabinett (formerly von Beckerath Collection).

Pen and light yellow and brown ink, on white paper. 143 × 190 mm. Signed and dated at upper left corner, BRVEGEL, *1561*.

This sheet was engraved by J. de Gheyn in 1598 (Bastelaer, *Estampes*, No. 94). Together with the following drawings it belongs to a series in which the theme is the romance of ruined castles.

Lit.: *Bastelaer*, No. 26; *Friedländer*, p. 187; Bock-Rosenberg, *Berlin Catalogue*, No. 5765; *Tolnay II*, No. 36.

39 : Plate 38

LANDSCAPE WITH RUINED CASTLE AND ROCKY GATEWAY. Vienna, Albertina.

Pen and light and darker brown ink, on white paper. Preliminary drawing in black chalk. 159 × 203 mm. Signed and dated at centre of upper margin, *Bruegel 1561*.

Lit.: *Bastelaer*, No. 28; Benesch, *Albertina Catalogue*, Vol. II (1928), No. 80; *Tolnay II*, No. 35.

40 : Plate 39

RUINED CASTLE AND CHAPEL ON ROCKY HILL. Berlin, Kupferstichkabinett (formerly von Beckerath Collection).

Pen and very light brown ink, on white paper. Cut at bottom. 97 × 194 mm. Signed and dated at centre of lower margin, *bruegel 1561* (half cut away in the middle).

Lit.: *Bastelaer*, No. 27; *Friedländer*, p. 186; Bock-Rosenberg, *Berlin Catalogue*, No. 5768; *Tolnay II*, No. 34.

41 : Plate 40

SUNRISE OVER A VALLEY. Paris, Louvre.

Pen and brownish-yellowish ink, on white paper. 143 × 185 mm. Signed and dated (in darker brown ink) at centre of upper margin, P BRVEGEL *1561*. Not well preserved. Watermark, a snake.

This drawing, which is among the most important of Bruegel's small landscapes, already reminds us in many respects of his painting *The Conversion of St. Paul*.

Lit.: *Bastelaer*, No. 25; *Michel*, pl. 76; *Ebbinge Wubben*, No. 46; *Tolnay II*, No. 38.

42 : Plate 41

WILDERNESS OF ROCKS WITH GORGE AND CASTLE. Rotterdam, Boymans-van Beuningen Museum.

Pen and yellowish ink, which is slightly darker in parts of the foreground, and is in barely visible, very light tones, in the background; on white paper. 160 × 209 mm. Signed and dated at upper left corner, BRVEGEL *1561*. The S below this added later in darker ink.

Tolnay rightly points out that Bruegel had used individual motifs of this landscape before. The choice of these is typical of a whole group of such small landscape sheets. The style of this drawing is closely related to that of the following.

Lit.: Museum Boymans, *Jaarvereslag*, 1938, p. 4; *Tolnay II*, No. 37.

43 : Plate 42

LANDSCAPE WITH A CASTLE. Besançon, Musée des Beaux-Arts (J. Gigoux Bequest).

Pen and yellowish and brown ink, on white paper. 198 × 311 mm. Signed and dated at centre of lower margin, *bruegel 1561*.

Tolnay, in my opinion wrongly, does not accept the authenticity of this free drawing. To me it seems particularly interesting, because with it Bruegel again returns to a larger format for his landscape drawings.

Lit.: *Tolnay II*, No. A17. [Translator's note: Tolnay published this drawing as authentic in 1960, in *Remarques sur quelques Dessins de Bruegel l'Ancien, Musées Royaux des Beaux Arts Bulletin*, 1960, 1-2, p. 18, fig. 11.]

44 : Plate 43

ROCKY LANDSCAPE WITH FORTRESS-CASTLE AT THE LEFT. Munich, Kupferstichkabinett.

Pen and ink, in very light and somewhat darker tones of brown, on white paper. Crease down the centre. 192 × 312 mm. Signed and dated at centre of upper margin, *bruegel 1562*.

Here, as in the following drawing, the style of Bruegel's 'universal landscapes', to which he returned in 1562, is clearly seen.

Lit.: *Bastelaer*, No. 29; *Ebbinge Wubben*, No. 47; *Tolnay II*, No. 39.

45 : Plate 44

LANDSCAPE WITH A VILLAGE. Brunswick, Herzog Anton Ulrich Museum.

Pen and ink, in lighter and darker tones of brown, on white paper. 180 × 310 mm. Signed and dated at centre of lower margin, *bruegel 1562*.

Lit.: *Tolnay II*, No. 40.

46 : Plate 45

THE BLIND MEN. Berlin, Kupferstichkabinett.

Pen and lighter and darker brown ink. 192×310 mm. Signed and dated at upper right corner, *bruegel 1562*.

This drawing with the blind men has here been placed among the landscapes of 1562, as it belongs to them in all its stylistic elements.

Lit.: *Bastelaer*, No. 97; *Hausenstein*, p. 74; *Friedländer*, p. 141; *Michel*, pl. 85; Bock-Rosenberg, *Berlin Catalogue*, No. 1376; *Tolnay II*, No. 65.

47 : Plate 46

TOWERS AND GATES OF AMSTERDAM. Besançon, Musée des Beaux-Arts.

Pen and yellowish and brown ink, on white paper. 183×304 mm. Signed and dated at lower right corner, *bruegel 1562*.

According to C. P. van Eeghen this, and the following two drawings, represent parts of the Amsterdam city walls.

Lit.: C. P. van Eeghen, *Poorten een Torens van Amsterdam*, in *Ochtenblad, Algemeen Handelsblad*, December 3, 1935; *Tolnay II*, No. 41.

48 : Plate 47

TOWERS AND GATES OF AMSTERDAM. Besançon, Musée des Beaux-Arts.

Pen and light and darker brown ink, on white paper. 183× 295 mm. Signed and dated at lower left corner, P. BRVEGEL *1562*.

Lit.: C. P. van Eeghen, *op. cit.*; *Tolnay II*, No. 42.

49 : Plate 48

TOWERS AND GATES OF AMSTERDAM. Boston (Mass.), Museum of Fine Arts.

Pen and yellowish ink, on white paper. 185×307 mm. Signed and dated at lower left corner, P BRVEGEL *1562*.

Lit.: *Catalogue of the R.W.P. de Vries Sale*, Amsterdam, March 27, 1925; C. P. van Eeghen, *op. cit.*; *Tolnay II*, No. 43.

50 : Plate 49

MARINE LANDSCAPE WITH A VIEW OF ANTWERP IN THE BACKGROUND. London, Count Antoine Seilern Collection.

Pen and ink, in several tones of brown, on white paper; slight traces of preliminary drawing in black chalk. 203×300 mm. The signature at lower left corner is not genuine.

Popham, who was the first to publish this drawing, rightly pointed out that it cannot have been executed before 1559. Although I cannot agree with Popham's suggested reading of the lines on the left as the date 1559, I have always believed this to be a late work. Benesch and Seilern have now also come to agree with this late dating – which I have always taken for granted – because of the close relationship of this sheet to the series of drawings of ships, some of which are dated 1565. Grossmann also agrees. With its deliberate use of several shades of ink and the remarkably lively use of the darker diagonal hatching, this drawing is a clear example of Bruegel's late style. The *Landscape with Storm at Sea* at Vienna is very close to the present drawing in its composition.

Lit.: A. E. Popham, *Old Master Drawings*, Vol. 9, No. 36, March 1935, p. 64, pl. 66; Benesch, *Kunstchronik*, 1953, p. 78; *Tolnay II*, No. 1; Seilern, *Catalogue*, No. 11; Grossmann, *Bulletin Boymans Museum, loc. cit.*

"NAER HET LEVEN"

51 : Plate 50

THREE PEASANT FIGURES, AND SKETCH OF A HAT. (*Recto* of No. 52.) Berlin, Kupferstichkabinett.

Pen and brown ink over preliminary drawing in black chalk, on reddish-white paper. 182×141 mm. Inscribed below on the left, *nart leven*. Numerous colour indications. About 1553–1556.

Already in his article in the 1929 *Jahrbuch* Tolnay corrected his error in rejecting this and the following sheets from Bruegel's work, though the date which he suggests for them, 1557/58, is too late. The *verso* of this sheet (our No. 52) makes it possible to date this group from about 1553 onwards.

Lit.: *Bastelaer*, No. 44; *Hausenstein*, p. 73; Tolnay, *J.d.pr.K.*,

1929, p. 213; Bock-Rosenberg, *Berlin Catalogue*, No. 729; *Tolnay II*, No. 70.

52 : Plate 52

STAG. (*Verso* of No. 51.) Berlin, Kupferstichkabinett.

Red chalk. 182×141 mm. About 1553.

The red chalk drawing is barely visible. The large drawing *Landscape with Town and St. Jerome* (our No. 22) has a stag in a very similar posture, so that it can hardly be wrong to date this drawing so early. The inscription *H. Bosch* is a later addition.

Lit.: Bock-Rosenberg, *Berlin Catalogue*, No. 729; *Tolnay II*, No. 120.

53 : Plate 53

BUFFALO. (*Verso* of No. 54.) Berlin, Kupferstichkabinett.

Black chalk. 187×145 mm. The inscription *H. Bosch*, in the upper right corner, is a later addition.

This sheet is also very delicately drawn, and the reproduction rather tends to exaggerate the line.

Lit.: Bock-Rosenberg, *Berlin Catalogue*, No. 733; *Tolnay II*, No. 121.

54 : Plate 51

BURGHER SEEN FROM THE BACK. (*Recto* of No. 53.) Berlin, Kupferstichkabinett.

Pen and brown ink over preliminary drawing in black chalk. 187×145 mm. Inscribed below at the centre, *Naert leven*. Several colour indications.

Lit.: *Bastelaer*, No. 55; *Friedländer*, p. 14; Bock-Rosenberg, *Berlin Catalogue*, No. 733; *Tolnay II*, No. 72.

55 : Plate 54

SEATED BURGHER AND CRIPPLE. (*Verso* of No. 56.) London, Count Antoine Seilern Collection.

Pen and lighter and darker brown ink over preliminary drawing in black chalk. 189×152 mm. Several colour indications. About 1553–55.

In his catalogue (No. 7) Seilern rightly points out that this drawing must have been executed earlier than 1557–58 (Tolnay), and he dates it between 1552 and 1555. It was obviously drawn shortly after the artist's return from Italy in 1553, or during his journey home.

Lit.: *Tolnay II*, No. 73; Seilern, *Catalogue*, No. 7.

56 : Plate 55

SEATED BURGHER. (*Recto* of No. 55.) London, Count Antoine Seilern Collection.

Pen and lighter and darker brown ink over preliminary drawing in black chalk. 189×152 mm. Inscribed below, near centre, *Nart leven*. *Pet Bruegell* at lower right corner is a later addition. Several colour indications. About 1553–55.

Compared to the preliminary chalk drawing visible underneath, part of the figure is rather coarsely executed, with an exaggeration, as for example in the nose, bordering on caricature. Seilern believes that as the boots are not completely visible the sheet must have been cut, especially at the left corner, but in its dimensions it corresponds so closely to the other early drawings, that this shortening can hardly have been substantial.

Lit.: *Tolnay II*, No. 74; Seilern, *Catalogue*, No. 7.

57 : Plate 56

WALKING PEASANT WITH HOE ON HIS SHOULDER. (*Recto* of No. 58.) Berlin, Kupferstichkabinett.

Pen and brown ink over preliminary drawing in black chalk, on reddish-white paper. 190×142 m m. Two colour indications. After 1556 – about 1558.

Compared to the impetuous writing on the earliest sheets, the inscriptions on this drawing already show a quieter handwriting. Only a part of the drawing has been outlined in ink. Tolnay rejects it.

Lit.: *Bastelaer*, No. 54; Bock-Rosenberg, *Berlin Catalogue*, No. 727; *Tolnay II*, No. A22.

58 : Plate 57

SEATED PEASANT SEEN FROM THE FRONT. (*Verso* of No. 57.) Berlin, Kupferstichkabinett.

Pen and dark brown ink over preliminary drawing in black chalk, on reddish-white paper. 190×142 mm. Inscribed in lighter ink, below at centre, *nart leven*. Several colour indications. About 1558.

The dating of the *recto* and *verso* of this sheet is determined by the relationship with the prisoner on the right of the large drawing *Charitas* (our No. 143), which is dated 1559. The way in which the eyes are especially emphasized is characteristic of Bruegel, right up to his late period (compare the two beggars in Berlin, our No. 118).

Lit.: *Bastelaer*, No. 48; Bock-Rosenberg, *Berlin Catalogue*, No. 727; *Tolnay II*, No. A23.

59 : Plate 58

TWO MARKET WOMEN. (*Verso* of No. 60.) Berlin, Kupferstichkabinett.

Pen and dark brown ink over preliminary drawing in black chalk, on reddish-white paper. 187×152 mm. Inscribed in lighter ink, below at centre, *nart leven*. Several colour indications. Watermark, two towers. About 1558.

Lit.: *Bastelaer*, No. 38; *Friedländer*, p. 146; Bock-Rosenberg, *Berlin Catalogue*, No. 728; *Tolnay II*, No. 71.

60 : Plate 59

PEASANT AND PEASANT WOMAN. (*Recto* of No. 59.) Berlin, Kupferstichkabinett.

Pen and brown ink over preliminary drawing in black chalk, on reddish-white paper. Only partially inked in. 187×152 mm. Inscribed in lighter ink, below at centre, *naert leven*. Several colour indications. Watermark, two towers. About 1558.

Tolnay's opinion, that the pen outline is not by Bruegel himself, is wrong.

Lit.: *Bastelaer*, No. 41; *Hausenstein*, p. 72; *Friedländer*, p. 30; Bock-Rosenberg, *Berlin Catalogue*, No. 728; *Tolnay II*, No. 76.

61 : Plate 60

FRONT AND SIDE VIEW OF A STANDING MAN. Weimar, Staatliche Kunstsammlungen, Schlossmuseum.

Pen and brown ink over preliminary drawing in black chalk. 155×118 mm. Several colour indications. About 1558.

Many years ago L. Burchard drew my attention to the existence of a series of drawings by Pieter Bruegel in Weimar. For the photograph of this drawing I am indebted to Dr. Scheidig, Director of the Weimar collection. In its style this drawing is so close to the preceding one that I feel justified in including it among Bruegel's original drawings, although the handwriting of the colour indications does not completely correspond with that on the other drawings of this group.

62 : Plate 61

MAN WITH LARGE BOOTS SEEN IN PROFILE. (*Recto* of No. 63.) Berlin, Kupferstichkabinett.

Pen and brown ink over preliminary drawing in black chalk, on reddish-white paper. Only partially inked in. 190×147 mm. Inscribed near lower left corner, *naert leven*. Several colour indications. About 1558-59.

The way in which, in the preliminary chalk sketch, the out-stretched hand has been re-drawn several times, is typical for Bruegel and his rapid assimilation of changes of movement. Especially in his animal drawings two or three changes in the position of one limb are often to be found. Judging by the inscription the drawing could also have been executed a little earlier.

Lit.: *Bastelaer*, No. 62; *Friedländer*, p. 147; Bock-Rosenberg, *Berlin Catalogue*, No. 732; *Tolnay II*, No. A39.

63 : Plate 63

MARKET WOMAN SEEN FROM THE FRONT. (*Verso* of No. 62.) Berlin, Kupferstichkabinett.

Pen and brown ink over preliminary drawing in red chalk, on reddish-white paper. 190×147 mm. About 1558-59.

Only the part of the figure outlined with the pen is visible. As opposed to the *recto* (our No. 62) Tolnay accepts this drawing, which is also not completed, as the work of Bruegel. According to my notes traces of red chalk drawing, and not black chalk, are visible.

Lit.: *Bastelaer*, No. 32; Bock-Rosenberg, *Berlin Catalogue*, No. 732; *Tolnay II*, No. 75.

64 : Plate 64

STUDY OF A HORSE. (*Verso* of No. 65.) Berlin, Kupferstichkabinett.

Chalk; snout and hind quarters in dark chalk. 158×95 mm. About 1558-59.

Lit.: *Bastelaer*, No. 80; Bock-Rosenberg, *Berlin Catalogue*, No. 723; *Tolnay II*, No. 122.

65 : Plate 65

PEASANT WOMAN WITH MILK JUG. (*Recto* of No. 64.) Berlin, Kupferstichkabinett.

Pen and brown ink, over preliminary drawing in black

chalk. 158×95 mm. Inscribed at lower right corner, *nart het leven*. Several colour indications. About 1558-59.

Tolnay only accepted this drawing in the second edition of his book, but he seems to me to have dated it too late. Like the preceding drawings this sheet belongs to a group which can be dated to about 1558-59.

Lit.: *Bastelaer*, No. 33; *Friedländer*, p. 165; Bock-Rosenberg, *Berlin Catalogue*, No. 723; *Tolnay II*, No. 78.

66 : Plate 62

A RICH PEASANT WOMAN, SEEN IN THREE-QUARTER PROFILE. The Hague, Le Clerq Collection.

Pen and yellowish ink over preliminary drawing in black chalk. 155×99 mm. At left lower corner a later inscription, in dark ink, *R. Savery*. Numerous colour indications. About 1559.

This peasant woman seen in three-quarter profile is richly dressed, though Tolnay's suggestion that it is oriental attire seems to me misleading. The sheet is inscribed below *R. Savery*, and this has led many scholars wrongly to attribute it to that artist. The handwriting of the colour indications, however, particularly points to its being an authentic work by Bruegel. Grossmann also agrees with this opinion.

Lit.: *Tolnay II*, addenda 1, repr. No. 81a; Grossmann, *op. cit.*

67 : Plate 66

STANDING MARKET WOMAN SEEN FROM THE BACK. (*Recto* of No. 68.) Frankfurt am Main, Städelsches Kunstinstitut.

Pen and brown ink over preliminary drawing in chalk. 157×103 mm. Inscribed at lower left corner, *nart het leven*. Several colour indications. About 1558-59.

This drawing, rejected by Tolnay, was published for the first time, not by him, but in *Stift und Feder*, 1926-27.

Lit.: *Bastelaer*, No. 34; *Stift und Feder*, Frankfurt a/M, 1926-27; *Tolnay II*, No. A.30.

68 : Plate 67

STANDING MAN WITH AN AXE UNDER HIS ARM, SEEN FROM THE BACK. (*Verso* of No. 67.) Frankfurt am Main, Städelsches Kunstinstitut.

Pen and brown ink over preliminary drawing in black chalk. The water-colours are a later addition. 157×103 mm. Inscribed at lower right corner, *nart het leven*. Numerous colour indications. About 1558-59.

Wrongly rejected by Tolnay.

Lit.: *Bastelaer*, No. 51; *Tolnay II*, No. A29.

69 : Plate 68

FIGURE ENVELOPED IN A PADDED CLOAK, SEEN FROM THE BACK. (*Recto* of No. 70.) Portinscale, Cumberland,

F. Springell Collection (formerly Liechtenstein Collection).

Pen and yellowish ink over preliminary drawing in black chalk. 160×100 mm. Inscribed below at centre, *nart het leven*. Several colour indications. About 1558–60.

Formerly in the Liechtenstein Collection, this drawing was acquired by Colnaghi's of London, and is now at Portinscale, Cumberland. Tolnay's doubts as to the authenticity of this sheet appear to me to be unfounded. As Mr. Byam Shaw informed me in a letter in March 1956, Tolnay retracted his doubts after seeing the original drawing.

Lit.: Schönbrunner-Meder, *Handzeichnungen alter Meister aus der Albertina*, No. 92b; *Bastelaer*, No. 59; *Tolnay II*, No. A27; P. & D. Colnaghi, London, *Exhibition Catalogue*, 12.5. – 27.6. 1953, No. 4.

70 : Plate 69

PEASANT SEEN IN PROFILE, WITH HIS LEFT HAND ON A WOODEN FENCE. (*Verso* of No. 69.) Portinscale, Cumberland, F. Springell Collection (formerly Liechtenstein Collection).

Pen and yellowish ink over preliminary drawing in chalk. The wash clearly added later. 160×100 mm. Inscribed below at centre, *nart het leven*. Several colour indications. About 1559–60.

The handwriting of the colour indications agrees so completely with that on accepted Bruegel's that any doubts as to the authenticity of this sheet seem to me unjustified.

Lit.: Schönbrunner-Meder, *Handzeichnungen alter Meister aus der Albertina*, No. 92a; *Bastelaer*, No. 60; *Tolnay II*, No. A28; P. & D. Colnaghi, *Exhibition Catalogue*, 12.5. to 27.6. 1953, No. 4.

71 : Plate 70

FIGURE IN A RAGGED CLOAK. (*Verso* of No. 72.) Frankfurt am Main, Städelsches Kunstinstitut.

Pen and light brown ink. 158×101 mm. Inscribed at lower left corner, *nart het leven*. Several colour indications. About 1559–63.

Despite its several weaknesses this drawing, like the preceding ones, should be included among the authentic works. It was reproduced for the first time not by Tolnay, but in *Stift und Feder*, 1926–1927.

Lit.: *Bastelaer*, No. 46; *Stift und Feder*, Frankfurt a/M, 1926–1927; *Tolnay II*, No. A26.

72 : Plate 71

WALKING MAN ENVELOPED IN A CLOAK. (*Recto* of No. 71.) Frankfurt am Main, Städelsches Kunstinstitut.

Pen and brown ink. The water-colours added later. 158×101 mm. Inscribed at lower left corner, *nart het leven*. Several colour indications. About 1559–63.

This drawing is also rejected by Tolnay.

Lit.: *Bastelaer*, No. 61; *Tolnay II*, No. A25.

73 : Plate 72

PEASANT WOMAN WITH HOE UNDER HER ARM AND BASKET ON HER BACK. (*Recto* of No. 74.) Stockholm, National Museum.

Pen and brown ink over preliminary drawing in black chalk. 160×102 mm. Inscribed at lower left corner, *nart het leven*. Several colour indications. After 1559–1563.

Like the *verso* this drawing has the more delicate line and the small handwriting which is characteristic of the late period.

Lit.: *Bastelaer*, No. 35; *Michel*, pl. 102; *Ebbinge Wubben*, No. 57; *Catalogue of Dutch and Flemish Drawings*, Stockholm 1953, No. 35; *Tolnay II*, No. 79.

74 : Plate 73

PEASANT WOMAN WITH BASKET ON HER BACK, SEEN IN QUARTER PROFILE. (*Verso* of No. 73.) Stockholm, National Museum.

Pen and brown ink with delicate inner drawing over black chalk. 160×102 mm. Several colour indications. About 1559–63.

Lit.: *Catalogue of Dutch and Flemish Drawings*, Stockholm 1953, No. 35; *Tolnay II*, No. 80.

75 : Plate 74

SEATED PEASANT WOMAN SEEN IN QUARTER PROFILE. (*Recto* of No. 76.) Uppsala, University Library.

Pen and brown ink over preliminary drawing in chalk. 154×99 mm. Inscribed below at centre, *nart het leven*. Several colour indications. Watermark indistinct. About 1559–63.

Lit.: *Catalogue of Dutch and Flemish Drawings*, Stockholm 1953, No. 38; Gunnar Ekholm, *Uppsala Universitetsbiblioteks Minneskrift*, 1621–1921, p. 582, repr. pl. 7; *Tolnay II*, No. 81.

76 : Plate 75

WALKING PEASANT SEEN FROM THE BACK. (*Verso* of No. 75.) Uppsala, University Library.

Chalk drawing. 154×99 mm. About 1559–63.

Nordenfalk was the first to mention this drawing, which, if I am not mistaken, is reproduced here for the first time. This sheet is important because it shows that in Bruegel's later works – as, for example, in the large picture *Autumn* – memories of drawings, which were executed at an earlier date, recur.

Lit.: *Catalogue of Dutch and Flemish Drawings*, Stockholm 1953. No. 381. [Translator's note: This drawing was published after Dr. Münz's death by F. Grossmann in *New Light on Bruegel*, *The Burlington Magazine*, CI, September/October 1959, p. 346, fig. 48; and by J. G. van Gelder in *Pieter Bruegel Naer "Het Leven"*, *Musées Royaux des Beaux Arts Bulletin*, Brussels, 1–2, p. 32, fig. 4.]

77 : Plate 76

SEATED PEASANT, AND STANDING PEASANT WOMAN WITH BASKET ON HER BACK. (*Recto* of No. 78.) New Rochelle, N.Y., Curtis O. Baer Collection (formerly Liechtenstein Collection).

Pen and brown ink over preliminary drawing in black chalk. 100×142 mm. Inscribed below, to left of centre, *nar leven*. Several colour indications. The signature, *P. Bruegel*, is a later addition. About 1559.

Lit.: O. Kurz, *Drei Zeichnungen P. Brueghels des Aelteren*, in *Die graphischen Künste*, new series I (1936), p. 5; *Tolnay II*, No. 82.

78 : Fig. 2

CHALK STUDY OF A PEASANT TURNED TO LEFT AND OF A WOMAN SEEN FROM THE BACK. (*Verso* of No. 77.) New Rochelle, N.Y., Curtis O. Baer Collection (formerly Liechtenstein Collection).

Black chalk. 100×142 mm. About 1559.

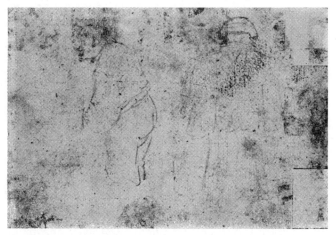

Fig. 2   Cat. No. 78

The back view of the woman, the type of her headgear and the kerchief beneath it, are so closely related to a woman at the fish-stall in Bruegel's painting *The Fight between Carnival and Lent* (fig. 25), that one can possibly date this drawing to the same year, 1559.

Lit.: *Tolnay II*, addenda 2; J. G. van Gelder, *loc. cit.*, p. 33, fig. 3.

79 : Plate 77

THREE PEASANT FIGURES, TWO SEEN FROM THE BACK, ONE IN PROFILE. Stockholm, National Museum.

Pen and yellowish ink over preliminary drawing in black chalk. Water stains in the paper. 170×197 mm. Inscribed below at centre, *nart het leven*. Numerous colour indications. About 1559–63.

Dr. Kurz has rightly pointed out that the seated peasant is identical with the peasant in drawing No. 77.

Lit.: *Bastelaer*, No. 77; Schönbrunner-Meder, *op. cit.*, No. 98; *Michel*, p. 163, note 1; *Ebbinge Wubben*, No. 58; *Cata-*

logue of Dutch and Flemish Drawings, Stockholm 1953, No. 37; O. Kurz, *op. cit.*; *Tolnay II*, No. 83.

80 : Plate 78

A SEATED AND A STANDING PEASANT. Berlin, Kupferstichkabinett.

Pen and brown ink over preliminary drawing in black chalk. Only touches of pen outline. 170×178 mm. Inscribed at lower left corner, *nart het leven*. Several colour indications. About 1559–63.

The postures of the seated and of the standing man are related to those in the preceding drawing, as is the delicate execution of the inner drawing.

Lit.: *Bastelaer*, No. 68; *Michel*, pl. 89; Bock-Rosenberg, *Berlin Catalogue*, No. 730; *Tolnay II*, No. 86.

81 : Plate 79

PEASANT SEEN FROM THE BACK, AND SOLDIER SEEN IN THREE-QUARTER RIGHT PROFILE. Berlin, Kupferstichkabinett.

Pen and rather light and darker brown ink over preliminary chalk drawing. 160×194 mm. Inscribed at lower left corner, *naert het leven*. Several colour indications. About 1559–63.

Although the use of a strong contrast between two inks often occurs, especially in the later drawings, Tolnay unaccountably rejects this drawing because one of the figures is executed in a darker shade of ink.

Lit.: *Bastelaer*, No. 70; Bock-Rosenberg, *Berlin Catalogue*, No. 731; *Tolnay II*, No. A38.

82 : Plate 80

THREE PEASANT FIGURES. Formerly in Paris, Heseltine-Richter Collection.

Pen and yellowish ink over preliminary drawing in black chalk. 164×194 mm. Inscribed below at centre, *nart het leven*. After 1560.

Like Tolnay, I know this drawing only from the reproduction in the auction catalogue, as it has now disappeared. Nevertheless, as far as I can judge its quality from the reproduction, I see no reason for considering it as only a copy, as Tolnay does.

Lit.: *Catalogue of the Heseltine-Richter Collection Sale*, Frederik Muller and Company, Amsterdam, 27–28 May, 1913, No. 68; *Tolnay II*, No. A36.

83 : Plate 81

TWO FIGURES IN HUNGARIAN COSTUME. Berlin, Kupferstichkabinett.

Pen and brown ink over preliminary drawing in black chalk. The water-colour added later 167×176 mm Inscribed at lower left corner, *nart het leven*. Numerous colour indications. About 1559–63.

The rider on the white horse in *The Procession to Calvary* of 1564 is wearing a very similar costume. Tolnay rejects not only the water-colour, but the whole drawing.

Lit.: *Bastelaer*, No. 71; Bock-Rosenberg, *Berlin Catalogue*, No. 5540; *Tolnay II*, No. A37a.

84 : Plate 82

THREE STUDIES, ON THE LEFT A CRIPPLE, ON THE RIGHT A SOLDIER. Rotterdam, Boymans-van Beuningen Museum.

Pen and light and dark brown ink over preliminary drawing in red chalk. 153×200 mm. Only a few of the numerous colour indications are outlined in pen. After 1560.

Tolnay's dating – after 1564 – is somewhat too late.

Lit.: Rooses, *De Teekeningen der Vlaamsche Meesters*, in *Onze Kunst*, I (1902), pp. 194 ff.; *Bastelaer*, No. 76; *Michel*, pl. 98; *Tolnay II*, No. 105.

85 : Plate 83

THREE STUDIES, IN THE CENTRE A SEATED BEGGAR SEEN IN PROFILE. Rotterdam, Boymans-van Beuningen Museum.

Pen and light ink over preliminary drawing in red chalk (like No. 84). 155×206 mm. Watermark, an eagle. Collector's mark on *verso*, MB. Inscribed below at centre, in very light ink, *naer het leven*. Several colour indications. False signature at lower right corner, *bruegel f.* About 1563–64.

Lit.: *Bastelaer*, No. 39; *Michel*, pl. 97; *Tolnay II*, No. 104.

86 : Plate 84

CRIPPLED BEGGAR. (*Recto* of No. 87.) Amsterdam, Rijksmuseum, Prentenkabinett.

Pen and pale ink, the face and shoes slightly darker; preliminary drawing in black chalk. 101×93 mm. Some colour indications. About 1563.

Lit.: *Bastelaer*, No. 52; *Michel*, pl. 94; *Tolnay II*, No. 100.

87 : Fig. 3

STAG STUDIES. (*Verso* of No. 86.) Amsterdam, Rijksmuseum, Prentenkabinett.

Black chalk. 101×93 mm. About 1563.

Several studies of moving stags. The sheet is a particularly charactcristic example of the way in which Bruegel quickly noted every change of movement. (Repr. on this page.)

Lit.: *Tolnay II*, No. 123.

88 : Plate 85

BURGHER SEEN FROM THE BACK. Vorden (Huize de Wiersse), Mme. A. Gatacre-de Stuers Collection.

Pen and darker and lighter brown ink over preliminary

drawing in chalk. 161×100 mm. Inscribed below at centre, *nart het leven*. Numerous colour indications. After 1564.

With its outlines in darker and lighter brown and its delicate inner drawing this example already belongs to the later sheets. [See Appendix No. 7 for the *verso* of this sheet.]

Lit.: *Bastelaer*, No. 57; *Michel*, p. 103, note; *Ebbinge Wubben*, No. 56; *Tolnay II*, No. 77.

89 : Plate 86

FOUR MEN STANDING IN CONVERSATION. Paris, Louvre.

Pen and brown ink. 210×150 mm. Inscribed below at centre: *Bruegel*. About 1560–63.

This is one of the few rapid pen drawings made by Bruegel without a preliminary sketch. The similarity of the figures to those in the *Justitia* (our No. 146) justifies us in considering the present drawing to be not much later than that sheet, that is about 1560–63, despite Tolnay's assumption that it was executed between 1565 and 1566.

Lit.: *Bastelaer*, No. 82; *Michel*, pl. 107; *Tolnay II*, No. 117.

90 : Plate 87

THE SHEPHERD. Dresden, Kupferstichkabinett.

Pen and light brown ink. 246×148 mm. About 1560–63.

As Bastelaer has already pointed out there is an exact copy of this large drawing in the Albertina at Vienna. The figure of the shepherd also recurs in paintings of the *Adoration of the Shepherds* by Jan Brueghel the Elder at Vienna.

Lit.: *Bastelaer*, No. 84; Woermann, *Handzeichnungen alter Meister in Dresden*, IV, pl. 11; *Michel*, pl. 106; *Tolnay II*, No. 116.

91 : Plate 88

TWO BURGHERS SEEN FROM THE BACK. Brussels, Bibliothèque Royale.

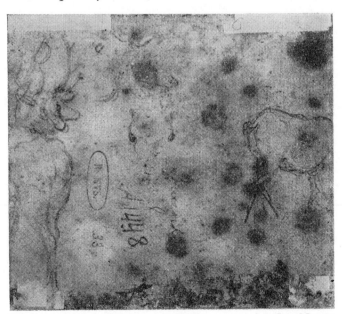

Fig. 3   Cat. No. 87

Pen and light and darker brown ink over preliminary drawing in black chalk. 156×139 mm. Watermark, two towers. Inscribed below at centre, *nart het leven*. Several colour indications. About 1564.

The way in which the drawing of the figure on the left is darker than that on the right is typical of the late period.

Lit.: *Bastelaer*, No. 75; *Bastelaer*, *Le dessin de P. Brueghel l'ancien appartenant au Cabinet des Estampes de la Bibliothèque Royale de Belgique, Societé des Bibliophiles et Iconophiles de Belgique*, Brussels, 1924; *Michel*, p. 102, pl. 90; *Ebbinge Wubben*, No. 59; *Tolnay II*, No. 88.

92 : Plate 89

TWO MEN SEEN FROM THE BACK. Weimar, Staatliche Kunstsammlungen, Schlossmuseum.

Pen and lighter and darker brown ink over preliminary chalk drawing. 158×167 mm. Inscribed at lower right corner, *nart het leven*. Several colour indications. After 1560.

The contrast between the outlines and the delicate inner drawing point to this sheet having been excuted after 1560, probably about 1564. For the photograph of this drawing, which Tolnay does not accept as authentic, I am indebted to Dr. Scheidig, Director of the State Collections in Weimar.

Lit.: *Handzeichnungen alter Meister im Grossherzoglichen Museum zu Weimar, Prestelgesellschaft*, 1913, I, No. 19; *Tolnay II*, No. A24.

93 : Plate 90

YOUNG PEASANT SEEN FROM THE BACK, AND OLDER PEASANT SHOWN IN HALF-LENGTH. Formerly Vienna, Liechtenstein Collection.

Pen and yellowish ink over preliminary drawing in black chalk. 168×158 mm. Inscribed at lower left corner, *nart het leven*. Several colour indications. About 1564–65.

Dr. Kurz was the first to publish this drawing, and I am indebted to him for the use of the photograph.

Lit.: O. Kurz, *Drei Zeichnungen P. Brueghel des Aelteren, Die graphischen Künste*, new series I (1936), p. 4; *Tolnay II*, No. 87.

94 : Plate 91

TWO WOODCUTTERS SEEN FROM THE BACK. Berlin, Kupferstichkabinett.

Pen and brown ink over preliminary drawing in black chalk. 135×137 mm. Inscribed at lower right corner, *nart het lev*(en). Several colour indications. Watermark, two towers. About 1565.

The small sketch of a figure on the right represents a dancing peasant, and not, as Tolnay presumed, a kneeling figure. Thus this is a study or first sketch, certainly dating from after 1560 and probably from about 1565, for a dancing peasant.

Lit.: *Friedländer*, p. 43; *Michel*, pl. 93; *Bock-Rosenberg, Berlin Catalogue*, No. 4434; *Tolnay II*, No. 97.

95 : Plate 92

TWO SPECTATORS. (*Verso* of No. 96.) Rotterdam, Boymans-van Beuningen Museum.

Pen and yellowish ink over preliminary drawing in black chalk. 153×96 mm. Some colour indications. 1564.

The disturbing over-drawing, which was still to be seen in Tolnay's reproduction, has now been removed. While the figure on the left has been partly outlined with the pen, in that on the right only the preliminary chalk drawing is to be seen. Of the two figures, that on the right can be considered as a study for one of the spectators in *The Carrying of the Cross* of 1564 (see fig. 24), and thus both drawings (*recto* and *verso*) probably date from this time.

Lit.: *Bastelaer*, No. 67; *Tolnay II*, No. 95.

96 : Plate 93

PEASANT YOUTH SEEN FROM THE BACK. (*Recto* of No. 95.) Rotterdam, Boymans-van Beuningen Museum.

Pen and light yellowish ink over very delicate preliminary chalk drawing, only the face being slightly darker. 153×96 mm. Some colour indications. 1564.

Lit.: *Bastelaer*, No. 63; *Tolnay II*, No. 94.

97 : Plate 94

TWO MARKET WOMEN. Rotterdam, Boymans-van Beuningen Museum.

Pen and light yellowish ink over preliminary drawing in black chalk. 151×100 mm. Inscribed below, at centre, *nart het leven*. Colour indications. About 1564.

The outlines have only been partially drawn with the pen, and here special stress has been laid on the accentuation of the faces of the two market women. The expression of greediness is much more strongly emphasized by the strokes of the pen than in what is visible of the preliminary drawing. The inscriptions, including the *nart het leven* below, are in light ink. The fragment of a basket in the upper right corner shows that the sheet was reduced to its present size at a later date.

Lit.: *Bastelaer*, No. 37; *Tolnay II*, No. 96.

98 : Plate 95

SEATED OLD PEASANT WOMAN, SEEN IN PROFILE. Rotterdam, Boymans-van Beuningen Museum.

Pen and light yellow-brown ink over preliminary drawing in black chalk. Damp stains. 127×109 mm. Some colour indications. Watermark, a tower (? fragment of the watermark of No. 91). About 1564.

Only a few of the outlines have been drawn with the pen, and they combine with the chalk drawing to form a delicate unity. Not all of the colour indications have been outlined in ink. On the *verso* there are trial pen strokes in brown ink.

Lit.: *Bastelaer*, No. 36; *Michel*, pl. 88; *Tolnay II*, No. 84.

99 : Plate 97

THE BLIND BEGGAR. Dresden, Kupferstichkabinett.

Pen and yellowish ink over preliminary drawing in black chalk. 130×83 mm. Two colour indications. The signature, *P. Breugel fec.*, is not authentic. About or after 1564.

Although the character of the handwriting points rather to the period around 1560, in the contrast between the darker outlines and the delicate inner drawing, and in the moving expression of the blind beggar's face, this drawing seems to belong to the series of the late drawings dating from about and after 1564.

Lit.: *Bastelaer*, No. 45; Woermann, *Handzeichnungen alter Meister in Dresden*, No. 126; *Romdahl*, p. 127; *Michel*, pl. 92; *Tolnay II*, No. 99.

100 : Plate 96

AN OLD MINER. Stockholm, National Museum.

Pen and darker and lighter brown ink over preliminary drawing in black chalk. 155×116 mm. Inscribed at lower left corner, *naert het leven*. Several colour indications. Watermark, an eagle. About 1564.

In the Stockholm Catalogue this drawing is dated about 1559–63, but, like Tolnay, I believe that it may have been executed a little later.

Lit.: *Bastelaer*, No. 65; *Catalogue of Dutch and Flemish Drawings*, Stockholm 1953, No. 36; *Tolnay II*, No. 90.

101 : Plate 98

TWO FIGURES OF MOUNTAIN PEASANTS. Berlin, Kupferstichkabinett.

Pen and brown ink over preliminary drawing in black chalk. 174×144 mm. Inscribed at lower right corner, *nart het leven*. Several colour indications. About 1564.

The writing of the colour indications is related to that on No. 99, but, as in the latter, everything else points to a later date. The clothing does not seem to me to represent a festive costume, but rather the dress worn by mountain peasants.

Lit.: *Bastelaer*, No. 69; *Friedländer*, p. 19; Bock-Rosenberg, *Berlin Catalogue*, No. 5538; *Tolnay II*, No. 98.

102 : Plate 99

THE PILGRIM. Vorden (Huize de Wiersse), Mme A. Gatacre-de Stuers Collection.

Pen and yellowish ink over preliminary drawing in black chalk. 320×195 mm. Inscribed at lower left corner, *nart leven*. Several colour indications. About 1564.

This drawing, which has clearly been cut on the right-hand side, is the largest of the *naer het leven* sheets.

Lit.: *Bastelaer*, No. 64; *Michel*, pl. 104; *Ebbinge Wubben*, No. 61; *Tolnay II*, No. 85.

103 : Plate 100

TWO BURGHERS SEEN IN PROFILE. Zürich, Private Collection (formerly Liechtenstein Collection).

Pen and lighter and darker brown ink, over preliminary drawing in black chalk. 160×190 mm. Inscribed at lower right corner, *nart het leven*. Several colour indications. About 1564.

For the new photograph of this drawing I am indebted to Frau Dr. Marianne Feilchenfeldt, of Zürich.

Lit.: O. Kurz, *Drei Zeichnungen P. Brueghel des Aelteren, Die graphischen Künste*, new series I (1936), p. 6; *Tolnay II*, No. 89.

104 : Plate 101

THREE STUDIES OF PEASANTS. Berlin, Kupferstichkabinett.

Pen and lighter and darker brown ink, over preliminary drawing in black chalk. 155×200 mm. Inscribed at lower right corner, *nart het leven*. Several colour indications. About 1564.

This drawing has now been lost. It is reproduced here from a photograph which the late Dr. Friedländer kindly placed at my disposal.

Lit.: *Bastelaer*, No. 74; *Friedländer*, p. 140; *Michel*, pl. 101; Bock-Rosenberg, *Berlin Catalogue*, No. 5531; *Tolnay II*, No. 110.

105 : Plate 102

TEAM OF HORSES. Vienna, Albertina.

Pen and darker and lighter brown ink, over preliminary drawing in black chalk. 164×184 mm. Inscribed at lower left, *nart leven*. Several colour indications. About 1564?

A team of horses of the same kind is already to be found in the large drawing with the St. George's Gate (No. 140), dating from 1559, but nevertheless the masterly use of the lighter and darker strokes speaks for a later date of execution for the present drawing.

Lit.: *Bastelaer*, No. 79; Schönbrunner-Meder, *Handzeichnungen aus der Albertina*, No. 1029; *Hausenstein*, p. 76; Benesch, *Albertina Catalogue*, No. 81; *Michel*, pl. 91; *Ebbinge Wubben*, No. 55; *Tolnay II*, No. 93.

106 : Plate 104

A MULE IN HARNESS. (*Recto* of No. 107.) London, Count Antoine Seilern Collection (formerly Lionel Lucas Collection, London).

Pen and darker and lighter brown ink. Traces of the preliminary chalk drawing are visible. 100×156 mm. Inscribed at lower right corner, *nart het leven*. Some colour indications. About 1564 or later.

In many ways this drawing is stylistically identical to the preceding one (No. 105).

Lit.: *Sale Catalogue of the Collection of Claude and Lionel Lucas*, Christie's, 9 December, 1949, lot 64; *Tolnay II*, No. 92.

107 : Plate 103

PEASANT SEEN FROM THE BACK. (*Verso* of No. 106.) London, Count Antoine Seilern Collection (formerly Lionel Lucas Collection, London).

Pen and darker and lighter brown ink. Much of the preliminary drawing is visible. 100×156 mm. Inscribed at lower right corner, *nart het leven*. Several colour indications. 1564 or later.

Tolnay excluded this drawing on the *verso* of No. 106 from Bruegel's oeuvre, despite the fact that in the large scale of the figure it is clearly in keeping with Bruegel's late drawings. Lugt's doubts as to the authenticity of both the back and front of this sheet seem to me unjustified.

Lit.: *Sale Catalogue of the Collection of Claude and Lionel Lucas*, Christie's, 9 December, 1949, lot 64; *Tolnay II*, No. A37.

108 : Plate 105

THE 'HORSE-TRADER'. Frankfurt am Main, Städelsches Kunstinstitut (Inv. No. 764).

Pen and darker and very light brown ink over preliminary drawing in black chalk. 195×147 mm. Inscribed at lower right corner, *nar hedt leven*. Several colour indications. About 1563.

In the cap on the right one can see in what an extraordinary way Bruegel altered the existing chalk sketch when he outlined the drawing with the pen.

Lit.: *Bastelaer*, No. 49; *Michel*, pl. 103; *Tolnay II*, No. 113.

109 : Plate 106

THREE BURGHERS, ONE SEEN IN PROFILE, ONE FROM THE BACK, AND ONE IN THREE-QUARTER VIEW. Vorden (Huize de Wiersse), Mme A. Gatacre-de Stuers Collection.

Pen and slightly darker and light brownish-yellow ink over preliminary drawing in black chalk. 165×185 mm. Inscribed at lower left corner, *nart het leven*. Numerous colour indications. About 1563.

A figure closely related to the man on the left occurs in the following drawing. The figure on the left is also repeated in the obviously later copy in the Universitätsbibliothek at Göttingen (No. A38). This small drawing in Göttingen (82×98 mm.), which I know only from a photograph, is very coarsely drawn.

Lit.: *Bastelaer*, No. 78; *Michel*, pl. 103, note; *Ebbinge Wubben*, No. 60; *Tolnay II*, No. 91.

110 : Plate 107

TWO RABBIS. Frankfurt am Main, Städelsches Kunstinstitut.

Pen and rather darker brown ink with lighter inner drawing,

over preliminary drawing in black chalk. 197×155. Inscribed at centre of lower margin, *nar hedt leven*. Several colour indications. About 1563–64.

The lively modelling of the heads and bodies is achieved by the combination of the lighter and darker brown ink with the grey-black, barely overdrawn portions of the preliminary drawing.

Lit.: *Bastelaer*, No. 73; *Handzeichnungen alter Meister in Frankurt am Main*, Prestelgesellschaft, Vol. 1, No. 7; *Michel*, pl. f02; *Tolnay II*, No. 114.

111 : Plate 108

TWO PEASANTS, ONE IN PROFILE, THE OTHER SEEN FROM THE BACK. Rotterdam, Boymans-van Beuningen Museum (formerly D. G. van Beuningen Collection).

Pen and lighter and darker brown ink over preliminary drawing in black chalk. 179×128 mm. Some colour indications. Collector's mark at lower left corner, Wauters (Brussels). Damaged at lower right corner. After 1564.

The strongly contrasting colourfulness and more powerful modelling of the figure on the left, which is more in the foreground, are characteristic of the late period.

Lit.: Fred Lees, *The Art of the Great Masters*, London, 1913, p. 69, fig. 80; D. Hannema, *Catalogue of the D. G. van Beuningen Collection*, Rotterdam, 1949, No. 155; *Tolnay II*, No. 106.

112 : Plate 109

WALKING MAN. Frankfurt am Main, Städelsches Kunstinstitut.

Pen and darker and lighter brown ink, over preliminary drawing in black chalk. 157×115 mm. Some traces of the obviously erased preliminary chalk drawing and handwriting are visible. Similarly, near the right edge of the drawing a second figure can be seen; traces of the head and of the whole body are still recognizable. About 1564.

The unfavourable opinion of Tolnay and other scholars concerning this drawing, may be due to the fact that, owing to the later attempt to erase the preliminary drawing, it is somewhat lacking in cohesion. But on closer examination the use of the lighter and darker brown ink is evident, and this alone would certainly tend to prove the authenticity of the drawing.

Lit.: *Bastelaer*, No. 50; *Tolnay II*, No. A33.

113 : Plate 110

MAN WITH A STAFF. Frankfurt am Main, Städelsches Kunstinstitut.

Pen and darker and lighter brown ink. Traces of the preliminary drawing in black chalk still clearly visible (rim of the cap). 157×100 mm. About 1564.

This drawing is also one of those in which the preliminary chalk drawing has been largely erased, and which, owing to the consequent tendency to lack inner cohesion, has been rejected, to my mind wrongly, by many scholars, including Tolnay. On the contrary the way in which the darker brown ink is here used to obtain contrast, as, for example, in the face, speaks for the authenticity of this drawing.

Lit.: *Bastelaer*, No. 47; *Friedländer*, p. 40; *Tolnay II*, No. A34.

114 : Plate 111

HALF-LENGTH FIGURE OF A PEASANT IN THREE-QUARTER PROFILE, LOOKING TO THE LEFT. Rotterdam, Boymans-van Beuningen Museum.

Pen and lighter and darker brown ink (face) over preliminary drawing in black chalk, which has been largely erased. Greyish-white paper. 191×139 mm. Inscribed at lower right corner, *nardt hedt leven.* Collector's mark at lower left corner, *C.E.* Some colour indications. On the *verso; provient de la collection d'Armand de Messrs. Saphorin.* About 1564–65.

This drawing, in which the handwriting certainly corresponds perfectly with that in Bruegel's original drawings, has been wrongly rejected by Tolnay, who claims to recognize the style of 1580 in the character of the line.

Lit.: *Catalogue de Ventes aux enchères Drouot*, 4 July, 1929, No. 18, Collection of Madame R. Blay; *Tolnay II*, No. A35.

115 : Plate 112

A MAN STANDING, SEEN FROM THE BACK. Weimar, Staatliche Kunstsammlungen, Schlossmuseum.

Pen and darker and lighter brown ink over preliminary chalk drawing. 188×116 mm. About 1565.

In its whole character this hitherto unpublished drawing, for the photograph of which I am indebted to Dr. Scheidig of Weimar, belongs to Bruegel's late drawings. Like many other drawings, it has not been entirely completed, and yet the corrections, as, for example, those on the right shoulder, show how much Bruegel developed the original chalk design. Traces of the colour indications which were obviously partly erased, are clearly visible, especially on the right by the cap, and, for example, near the hip and trousers.

116 : Plate 113

FIGURE WITH A TALL HAT SEEN FROM THE BACK; ON THE RIGHT, A SECOND FIGURE SEEN FROM THE BACK. Rotterdam, Boymans-van Beuningen Museum (formerly Koenigs Collection).

Pen and dark brown ink, with slightly lighter inner drawing, over preliminary drawing in black chalk. 194×123 mm. Inscribed at lower right corner, *nar hedt.* Some colour indications. After 1565.

Tolnay rightly points out that the fragmentary inscription at the lower right corner, *nar hedt,* shows that the sheet was subsequently cut. There is a copy of it in the Delacre Collection, Ghent (196×250 mm, No. A39), forming the right half of a sheet the left half of which shows two figures which must have belonged to a *naer het leven* study now lost. The manneristic marked accentuation of the upper part of the body occurs in much the same way on the Weimar drawing No. 115.

Lit.: *Ebbinge Wubben*, No. 68; *Tolnay II*, No. 103.

117 : Plate 114

BEGGAR WITH A TURBAN, AND STUDY OF A HEAD. Amsterdam, Rijksmuseum, Prentenkabinett.

Pen and darker and lighter brown ink (face somewhat darker) over preliminary drawing in red chalk. 147×137 mm. Inscribed at lower right corner, *nart het leven.* Several colour indications. Watermark, an inverted T. About 1565.

Lit.: *Bastelaer*, No. 53; *Michel*, pl. 95; *Tolnay II*, No. 101.

118 : Plate 115

TWO BEGGARS SEATED. Berlin, Kupferstichkabinett.

Pen and darker and lighter brown ink, over preliminary drawing in black chalk. 206×191 mm. Inscribed at lower margin, *nart leven.* Several colour indications. About 1565.

This exceptional late drawing, with the contrast between the darker outlines of the figure in front – the beggar holding the hat – and the figure behind, was rejected by Tolnay, at first completely and later partially. He amended his opinion in that he came to consider the preliminary chalk drawing as Bruegel's own, but not the outline. Particularly characteristic of Bruegel's authentic work, however, is the way in which the preliminary chalk drawing of the seated beggar in front has been altered during the further work on this sheet.

Lit.: *Bastelaer*, No. 66; *Friedländer*, p. 22; Bock-Rosenberg, *Berlin Catalogue*, No. 734; *Tolnay II*, No. A40.

119 : Plate 116

SEATED MAN SEEN FROM THE FRONT, AND HALF-LENGTH FIGURE TURNED THREE-QUARTERS TO RIGHT. Paris, F. Lugt Collection.

Pen and lighter and darker brown ink, over preliminary drawing in black chalk. 150×160 mm. Inscribed below at left, *nart het leven.* Several colour indications. Forged Dürer monogram at lower right corner. About or after 1565.

Published for the first time by Tolnay, this drawing belongs to the series of Bruegel's late drawings.

Lit.: *Tolnay II*, No. 107.

120 : Plate 117

TWO PEASANTS IN HALF-LENGTH. Cleveland, Museum of Art (J. H. Wade Collection 1945).

Pen and lighter and slightly darker brown ink, over preliminary drawing in black chalk. 151×188 mm. Inscribed to left of lower margin, *nart het leven*. Some colour indications. About or after 1565.

First published by Tolnay.

Lit.: *Michel*, pl. 99; Francis, *A Drawing by Pieter Bruegel the Elder*, Bulletin of the Cleveland Museum of Art, 33, 1946; *Tolnay II*, No. 112.

121 : Plate 118

SEATED PEASANT ASLEEP. Dresden, Kupferstichkabinett.

Pen and lighter and darker brown ink, over preliminary drawing in black chalk. 177×188 mm. Inscribed at lower right corner, *nart hed leven*. Some colour indications. About 1565.

This drawing has now been lost, and is reproduced here after Woermann, *Handzeichnungen alter Meister in Dresden*, No. 125.

Lit.: *Bastelaer*, No. 56; Woermann, *loc. cit.*; *Michel*, pl. 100; *Tolnay II*, No. 111.

122 : Plate 119

TWO SEATED PEASANT WOMEN, SEEN FROM THE BACK. Dresden, Kupferstichkabinett.

Pen and darker and lighter brown ink, over preliminary drawing in black chalk. 151×185 mm. Inscribed at lower left corner, *nart het leven*. Several colour indications. About 1565.

This drawing has also been lost and has had to be reproduced here from Woermann, *op. cit.*, No. 124. Particularly instructive for the study of Bruegel's late style is a comparison between this drawing and the studies of small figures showing the same motif, such as No. 59.

Lit.: *Bastelaer*, No. 40; Woermann, *loc. cit.*; *Tolnay II*, No. 115.

123 : Plate 120

PEASANT WOMAN, AND PEASANT SEEN FROM THE BACK, BOTH IN HALF-LENGTH. Amsterdam, Rijksmuseum, Prentenkabinett.

Pen and very light yellow ink, over preliminary drawing in black chalk. 126×100 mm. Several colour indications. Watermark; fragment of a clover-leaf. 1565 or later.

This drawing, in which the very economically applied pen outline in two tones blends perfectly with the preliminary chalk drawing, belongs to the most outstanding of Bruegel's drawings.

Lit.: *Bastelaer*, No. 42; *Michel*, pl. 96; *Ebbinge Wubben*, No. 62; *Tolnay II*, No. 102.

124 : Plate 121

PEASANT WOMAN SEEN FROM THE BACK. Berlin, Kupferstichkabinett.

Pen and darker and lighter brown ink, over preliminary drawing in black chalk, on reddish-white paper. 138×99 mm. Several colour indications. About 1565.

Lit.: *Friedländer*, p. 18; Bock-Rosenberg, *Berlin Catalogue*, No. 4948; *Tolnay II*, No. 109.

125 : Plate 122

SEATED PEASANT, SEEN IN PROFILE, WITH BASKET ON HIS LAP. Vienna, Albertina.

Pen and darker and slightly lighter brown ink, over preliminary drawing in black chalk. 158×152 mm. Inscribed near centre of lower margin, *nar hedt leven*. Some colour indications. About 1565 or later.

Lit.: *Bastelaer*, No. 58, repr. pl. 38; Benesch, *Albertina Catalogue*, No. 82; *Tolnay II*, No. 108.

126 : Plate 123

THE PAINTER AND THE CONNOISSEUR. Vienna, Albertina.

Pen and darker and lighter brown ink. 250×216 mm. (according to Benesch). Signature at lower left corner doubtful. About 1565 or later.

This late drawing is one of those which must have been highly esteemed very quickly, since four copies of it exist.

1. The drawing in the Vincent Korda Collection, London, 298×219 mm. which has a slightly larger blank area at the top and the bottom, and which is inscribed, on an attached piece of paper; *Effigies Jeronomi Bos ad vivum delineata a Pitro Breugelio discipulo suo Ao. 1537*. Despite its weaknesses, Tolnay reproduced this drawing, both in an article and later in his book under No. 119, as an authentic work by Bruegel. [Our No. A46.]

2. The rather coarse copy, cut at the top corners, in the British Museum. [Popham, *Catalogue*, V. p. 145, No. 8. Our No. A48.]

3. A copy formerly in the possession of Dr. Eberhard Kornfeld, Bern, inscribed *Jaques Savery*. [Sold Klipstein and Kornfeld, Bern, Auction 98, 16 June, 1960, lot 44, repr. pl. 24 – attributed to Bruegel. Our No. A45.]

4. The copy in the possession of the art-dealer Ch. Nebehay, Vienna, 272×216 mm., which is inscribed on the *verso* in an old hand: *von Hufnagel 1602*. Hœfnagel (born Antwerp 1542, died Vienna 1600) is known to have been one of the artists who were very familiar with Bruegel's work, especially as engravers and publishers of it. [Our No. A47.]

Lit.: *Bastelaer*, No. 104; *Romdahl*, p. 148, pl. XXIV; Schönbrunner-Meder, *Handzeichnungen alter Meister aus der Albertina*, No. 358; *Hausenstein*, p. 91; Meder, *Albertina Facsimile*, pl. IV; Benesch, *Albertina Catalogue*, No. 84; *Michel*, pl. 108; Benesch, *Northern Renaissance*, pp. 94 ff.; Tolnay, *Les Arts Plastiques*, 1948, pp. 455 ff.; *Ebbinge Wubben*, No. 42; *Tolnay II*, No. 118; Benesch, *Zur Frage der Kopien nach Pieter Bruegel*, Musées Royaux des Beaux Arts Bulletin, Brussels, 1959, 1–2, pp. 35 ff.; Tolnay, *Remarques sur quelques Dessins de Bruegel l'Ancien*, Musées Royaux des Beaux-Arts Bulletin, Brussels, 1960, 1–2, pp. 3 ff.

COMPOSITIONS

(DESIGNS FOR ENGRAVINGS)

127 : Plate 124

THE TEMPTATION OF ST. ANTHONY. Oxford, Ashmolean Museum.

Pen and slightly darker and lighter yellowish-brown ink, on brownish paper. 216×326 mm. The authenticity of the inscription *Brueggel 1556*, in darker ink at lower left corner, is doubted by K. T. Parker. Preliminary drawing in the same direction for the engraving, Bastelaer, *Estampes*, No. 119.

This drawing is the earliest surviving composition by Bruegel. It shows him so completely independent of Hieronymus Bosch, that doubts have been cast on its authenticity. No one has as yet succeeded in giving a complete explanation of the individual parts of this drawing. Parts of the composition, in particular the archer at the upper right corner shooting at a bird climbing out of a jug, are to be found in a painting of the Bosch School, *The Temptation of St. Anthony*, in the Galleria Colonna at Rome. Very similar versions of the Saint himself are found in drawings by Bosch. Tolnay suggests that the head, with smoke issuing from its mouth, is a so-called '*Peterskopf*', as mentioned in Murner's *Narrenbeschwörung*, chapter 85, and Fischart's *Flohhatz*. Without any closer explanation he identifies this head with the corrupt church – hollow inside, in accordance with the proverb, 'His head is as hollow as an empty egg-shell'. The smoke issuing from the mouth he relates to the proverb, 'When the head is full of smoke, no light can shine in it'. Tolnay connects the way in which the spectacles have grown through the nostril with the proverb, 'This is not a nose designed for wearing spectacles'. This interpretation seems to me just as doubtful as the other one, 'First the nose, and then the glasses', as a symbol of perversity. In the mouth there are two monks corresponding to the proverb, 'to make someone's head hot', that is to annoy somebody. The large fish above the head, with struggling human beings inside it, denotes, according to Tolnay, 'Don't let the herring swim over your head'. Tolnay believes that the document hanging from the branch of the tree growing out of the fish is a Papal Bull; while the fish itself signifies the Papacy, which rules the world. The interpretation of the man on the branch to the right, 'he has his head in a sack', seems to me to be nearer the real meaning. From the purely compositional point of view Tolnay's statement that the two figures in the foreground remind us of the *Fight between Carnival and Lent*, in Vienna, appears to be correct.

Lit.: *Bastelaer*, pp. 158 ff.; K. T. Parker, *Catalogue of the Collection of Drawings in the Ashmolean Museum*, 1938, Vol. I, No. 30, pl. VII; *Tolnay II*, No. 46.

128 : Plate 125

BIG FISH EAT LITTLE FISH. Vienna, Albertina.

Pen and greyish-black ink. 216×302 mm. Signed and dated at lower right corner, *1556 brueghel*. Preliminary drawing in reverse for Pieter van der Heyden's engraving, Bastelaer, *Estampes*, No. 139. In the first edition the engraving bore the inscription, *Hieronymus Bos inventor*.

The drawing is obviously to a great extent inspired by Hieronymus Bosch, and is probably a re-drawing by Bruegel after motifs by Bosch. It already shows Bruegel's fully developed style of drawing, as in the way in which in the large fish, in addition to the horizontal and vertical hatching, little curves are used to add life. The didactic elements of this drawing, with the men in the boat in the foreground, one of whom points to the large fish, the belly of which is being cut open by a soldier with a jagged knife, on which is the symbol of the world, belong to Bruegel's world. He might have drawn the inspiration for them from, among others, Bosch's *Last Judgement*, now in the Academy Gallery at Vienna. In the representation of the big fish, which finally has to yield up its prey – the little fish it has swallowed, some of which have still smaller fish in their mouths – it is all part of Bruegel's consequential thinking that, on the left, the man fishing with the little minnow as bait should illustrate the proverb: 'Big fish can be caught with little fish', or 'One fish can be caught with another'.

Lit.: *Bastelaer*, No. 90; *Romdahl*, p. 123; Burchard, *Amtliche Berichte*, XXXIV, cols. 224–6; *Friedländer*, pp. 62 ff.; *Michel*, pl. 78; Benesch, *Albertina Catalogue*, No. 76; Benesch, *Northern Renaissance*, pp. 93 ff.; *Tolnay II*, No. 44.

129 : Plate 126

THE ASS IN THE SCHOOL. Berlin, Kupferstichkabinett. (Formerly Fairfax Murray Collection.)

Pen and black ink, the inscription at the lower margin in brown. A damage in the face of the little monk to the right of the teacher. 232×307 mm. Signed and dated at lower left corner, *brueghel 1556*. Watermark, a jug with flowers and two letters.

The preliminary drawing, in reverse, for the engraving by Pieter van der Heyden (Bastelaer, *Estampes*, No. 142). The inscription below reads: *Al reyst den esele ter scholen om leeren – ist eenen esele hy en sal gheen peert weder keeren*. ('Although the ass goes to school to learn – this one here is (nevertheless) an ass and will never become a horse' – Tolnay's translation.) Since Brandt's *Narrenschiff*, to which

Tolnay draws attention, the ass as a teacher had been a favourite subject for humanistic illustrators.

Lit.: *Friedländer*, p. 45; *Michel*, pl. 77, p. 97; Bock-Rosenberg, *Berlin Catalogue*, No. 11641; *Tolnay II*, No. 45.

130 : Plate 127

AVARITIA. (First sheet of the series of The Vices.) London, British Museum.

Pen and blackish-brown ink. 228×297 mm. Signed and dated at lower right corner, *brueghel 1556*.

The preliminary drawing in reverse for Pieter van der Heyden's engraving (Bastelaer, *Estampes*, No. 128). Inscribed in a lighter ink, and in a different hand, beneath the central figure, *avaritia*; and along the lower margin, *Eere beleestheyt schaemte noch godlijck varmaen, En siet die scrapende gierichthyt niet aen*. ('Honour, courtesy (good breeding) shame and divine admonition are not regarded by grasping avarice' – Tolnay's translation.)

(Translator's note: Dr. Münz had intended to give detailed interpretations of this, and all the other sheets in the series of The Vices and Virtues, in the volume which he had planned to write on Bruegel's Engravings.)

Lit.: *Michel*, pp. 98 and 131; Popham, *Catalogue of Drawings by Dutch and Flemish Artists in the British Museum*, Vol. V, London 1932, p. 143, No. 4; J. van Gelder and Jan Borms, *Brueghels zeven deugden en zeven hoofdzonden*, Amsterdam-Antwerp (1939); J. B. F. van Gils, *Een andere kijk op Pieter Bruegel den Ouden*, The Hague, 1941, II, pp. 55 ff.; *Tolnay II* No. 47.

131 : Plate 128

GULA. Paris, F. Lugt Collection.

Pen and yellowish-brown ink. 230×302 mm. Signed and dated at lower right corner, *brueghel 1557*. Watermark: the Imperial double eagle.

The preliminary drawing in reverse for Pieter van der Heyden's engraving (Bastelaer, *Estampes*, No. 129). Inscribed beneath the central figure, *gula*; and along the lower margin, *Schout dronckenschap endt gulsichlijk eten – Want overdaet doet godt en hem selven vergethen*. ('Shun drunkenness and gluttony, for excess makes a man forget God and himself' – Tolnay's translation.) The inscription and the word '*gula*' are in another hand.

Lit.: *Friedländer*, p. 181; van Gelder and Borms, *op. cit.*; Van Gils, *op. cit.*; *Tolnay II*, No. 48.

132 : Plate 129

SUPERBIA. Paris, F. Lugt Collection.

Pen and brown ink. 230×300 mm. Signed and dated at lower left corner, *brueghel 1557*.

The preliminary drawing in reverse for Pieter van der Heyden's engraving (Bastelaer, *Estampes*, No. 127). Inscribed beneath the central figure, *Superbia*; and along the lower margin, *Hoouaerdye wert van godt bouen al ghehaet –*

Tseghelyc wert godt weder van hoouerdye versmaet. ('Pride is hated by God above and at the same time God is reviled by pride' – Tolnay's translation.) The inscription and the word '*Superbia*' are in another hand.

Lit.: *Friedländer*, p. 60; Van Gelder and Borms, *op. cit.*; Van Gils, *op. cit.*; *Tolnay II*, No. 49.

133 : Plate 130

LUXURIA. Brussels, Bibliothèque Royale.

Pen and brown ink. 226×297 mm. Signed and dated at lower right corner, *brueghel 1557*. Watermark, an Imperial eagle.

The preliminary drawing in reverse for Pieter van der Heyden's engraving (Bastelaer, *Estampes*, No. 131). Inscribed beneath the central figure, *luxuria*; and along the lower margin, *Luxurye stinckt sy is vol onsuyuerheden – Sy breeckts die crachten en sy swackt die leden*. ('Lechery stinks, it is full of uncleanness, it breaks the powers and weakens the limbs' – Tolnay's translation.) This inscription and the word '*Luxuria*' are in another hand.

Lit.: *Bastelaer*, No. 91; Bastelaer, *Les dessins de P. Brueghel l'ancien appartenant au Cabinet des Estampes de la Bibliothèque Royale de Belgique, Société des Bibliophiles et Iconophiles de Belgique*, Brussels, 1924; *Michel*, p. 98, pl. 78; Van Gelder and Borms, *op. cit.*; pl. 3; Van Gils, *op. cit.*, II, pp. 68–74; *Ebbinge Wubben*, No. 49; *Tolnay II*, No. 50.

134 : Plate 131

IRA. Florence, Uffizi.

Pen and brown ink. 230×300 mm. Signed and dated at lower left corner, *brueghel 1557*.

The preliminary drawing in reverse for Pieter van der Heyden's engraving (Bastelaer, *Estampes*, No. 125). Inscribed beneath the central figure, *ira*; and along the lower margin, *Gramschap doet den mout swillen en verbittert den moet– Sy beroert den geest en maeckt swert dat bloet*. ('Wrath makes the mouth swell and embitters the spirit, infects the mind, and makes the blood black' – Tolnay's translation.) The inscription and the word '*ira*' in another hand.

Lit.: *Bastelaer*, No. 92; *I disegni della R. Galleria degli Uffizi*, Florence, Olschki, 1915, III, Part 3, No. 21; Van Gelder and Borms, *op. cit.*; Van Gils, *op. cit.*; L. Münz, *Blick in die Welt*, London 1946/47, No. 1, pp. 38–9; *Tolnay II*, No. 51.

135 : Plate 132

INVIDIA. Basle, Baron R. von Hirsch Collection (formerly in the Collection of Count de Robiano).

Pen and dark brown (almost black) ink. 220×300 mm. Signed and dated at lower left corner, *brueghel 1557*.

The preliminary drawing in reverse for Pieter van der Heyden's engraving (Bastelaer, *Estampes*, No. 130). Inscribed beneath the central figure, *invidia*; and along the lower margin, *Een onsterffelycke doot es nyt en wreede peste –*

Een beest die haer selven eet met valschen moleste. ('Envy is an immortal death, an evil pestilence, a beast which devours itself with false care' – Tolnay's translation.) The inscription and the word '*invidia*' are in another hand.

Lit.: Sale Catalogue, *Collection E. Beurdeley*, Paris, 8–10 June, 1920, lot 6; Van Gelder and Borms, *op. cit.*; Van Gils, *op. cit.*; colour reproduction in the magazine *Du*, Zürich, 1951; *Tolnay II*, No. 52.

136 : Plate 133

DESIDIA. Vienna, Albertina.

Pen and blackish-brown ink. 214×296 mm. Signed and dated at lower right corner, *brueghel 1557*.

The preliminary drawing in reverse for Pieter van der Heyden's engraving (Bastelaer, *Estampes*, No. 126). The word *desidia*, beneath the central figure, in another hand and in lighter ink. Inscription (cut off and pasted on to the *verso*), *Trachheyt mackt machteloos en verdroocht – Die senuwen dat de mensch niewers toe en doocht.* ('Sloth makes powerless and dries out the nerves (sinews), so that the man is good for nothing'– Tolnay's translation.)

Lit.: *Bastelaer*, No. 93; *Romdahl*, p. 113, pl. 17; *Hausenstein*, p. 22; *Friedländer*, p. 64; Fraenger, *Der Bauern-Bruegel und das deutsche Sprichwort*, Zürich, 1923, p. 34; Benesch, *Albertina Catalogue*, No. 77; Van Gelder and Borms, *op. cit.*; Van Gils, *op. cit.*; *Tolnay II*, No. 53.

137 : Plate 134

THE LAST JUDGEMENT. Vienna, Albertina.

Pen and blackish-brown ink. 230×299 mm. Signed and dated at lower right corner, *brueghel 1558*. The preliminary drawing in reverse for Pieter van der Heyden's engraving (Bastelaer, *Estampes*, No. 121). Inscribed at the lower margin in another hand and in lighter bistre, *Compt ghy gebenedyde myns vaeders hier – En gaet ghy vermaldyde in dat eeuwighe vier.* ('Come here you who are blessed by my father. And you who are damned go to the eternal fires'.)

The attitude of Christ as Judge of the World, the angels with the long trumpets and the groups of Saints and Apostles at the upper left and right corners, are basically derived from Hieronymus Bosch. It is an essential element of Bruegel's conception, that, just as with Bosch, the devils are shown in a final struggle still to force the blessed back into hell. It is characteristic of the publisher Hieronymus Cock, that, in 1564, he published a Last Judgement, completely in the classical tradition, after Martin van Heemskerk.

Lit.: *Bastelaer*, No. 89; *Romdahl*, p. 111; Benesch, *Albertina Catalogue*, No. 78; *Tolnay II*, No. 54.

138 : Plate 135

'ELCK' OR 'EVERYMAN'. London, British Museum.

Pen and brownish ink, on reddish-discoloured white paper. The outlines are partially pressed through with a stylus. 210×293 mm. Signed and dated at lower left corner, *brueghel 1558*. Partially cut. Watermark, Imperial eagle. Preliminary drawing in reverse for Pieter van der Heyden's engraving (Bastelaer, *Estampes*, No. 152).

The figure of Everyman, who is always seeking the enemy outside, but never within, himself, was already the subject of large wood-cuts in Germany before Bruegel's time.

Lit.: *Bastelaer*, No. 96; *Michel*, Nos. 98 and 131, pl. 80; Popham, *Catalogue of Drawings by Dutch and Flemish Artists in the British Museum*, London 1932, V, p. 143, No. 3; *Tolnay II*, No. 55.

139 : Plates 136, 152

THE ALCHEMIST. Berlin, Kupferstichkabinett (Crozat Collection).

Pen and brown ink. 308×453 mm. Signed and dated at upper right corner, BRUEGHEL *1558*. Preliminary drawing in reverse for Pieter van der Heyden's engraving (Bastelaer, *Estampes*, No. 197). On the scholar's book, to the left, the inscription *Alghe-Mist* ('All is in Vain').

Tolnay doubts the authenticity of the signature at the upper right. Since Brandt's *Narrenschiff* the representation of the harm wrought by alchemy was one of the most popular themes of Renaissance satire. Most closely related to Bruegel is a drawing by Verbeecq, now in Constance, to which L. Goldscheider kindly drew my attention.

Lit.: Friedländer, *Bernaert van Orley*, in: *J.d.p.K.*, XXX, 1909, p. 153; *Friedländer*, p. 71; *Michel*, pl. 81; Bock-Rosenberg, *Berlin Catalogue*, No. 4399, pl. 13; *Tolnay II*, No. 56.

140 : Plate 137

SKATING OUTSIDE ST. GEORGE'S GATE. Private Collection in America.

Pen and lighter and darker brown ink. 213×298 mm. Signed and dated at lower right corner, *brueghel 1559*.

This drawing is the re-discovered preliminary drawing in reverse for Pieter van der Heyden's engraving (Bastelaer, *Estampes*, No. 205), and is here published for the first time. In its second state, from which the address of Cock has been removed, the engraving is erroneously inscribed, *P. Breugel delineavit et pinxit ad vivum 1553*. At this time the engraving was given a moral interpretation: *LUBRICITAS VITAE HUMANAE. LA LUBRICITE DE LA VIE HUMAINE. De Slibberachtigheyt van's Menschen Leven.* Gustav Glück, whose attention was drawn to it by Friedländer, was the first to describe this drawing. Like F. Grossmann, he reads the date as *1558*, and has no doubt that the last figure is an *8*. The doubts of Auner (note, p.75 of his article), who reads the last figure as a *3*, seem to me unjustified.

Li.: Gustav Glück, *Das grosse Breugel Werk*, Vienna 1951, No. 78, p. 111; Michael Auner, *Pieter Bruegel, Umrisse eines Lebensbildes, Jahrbuch d. Kunsthist. Samml. in Wien*, Vol. 52, 1956, pp. 51 ff.; F. Grossmann, *New Light on Bruegel*, *The Burlington Magazine*, CI, September-October 1959, p. 345.

141 : Plate 138

THE KERMESS OF HOBOKEN. Formerly London, Oppenheimer Collection (from the Mackenzie of Gairloch Collection).

Pen and brown ink. 265×394 mm. Signed and dated at lower left, *1559 BRVEGEL*. Preliminary drawing in reverse for the engraving, Bastelaer, *Estampes*, No. 208.

This drawing was originally published by Popham, when it was still in the Oppenheimer Collection, as a work by Pieter Bruegel (*Vasari Society*, Second Series, Vol. II, 1921, No. 12). Tolnay rejects its authenticity. Lebeer believes it to be a drawing by the engraver F.H.B. The fact that I have never seen the original of this drawing, the present owner of which is unknown to me, has made it more difficult for me to form an opinion on this sheet, but there are many reasons for thinking that it is a much-worn original. The style of the handwriting in the signature and date corresponds with that of Bruegel.

Lit.: Popham, *op. cit.*; *Oppenheimer Sale Catalogue*, Christie's, 13 July 1936, lot 223; *Tolnay II*, No. A20; Louis Lebeer, *Miscellanea Leo van Puyvelde*, Brussels 1949, p. 99.

142 : Plate 139

FIDES. (First sheet of the series of The Virtues.) Amsterdam, Rijksmuseum, Prentenkabinett.

Pen and brown ink, dark violet-brown in the shaded parts. 226×295 mm. Signed and dated at lower left corner, BRVEGEL *1559*. Preliminary drawing in reverse for the engraving probably by Philippe Galle (Bastelaer, *Estampes*, No. 132).

Unlike Tolnay, I think that the signature is authentic, even though the original signature in the lower right corner has been erased. The word FIDES and the inscription below it are in lighter ink and in another hand: *Fides maxime a nobis conservanda est praecipue in religionem, quia deus prior et potentior est quam homo.*

Lit.: *Michel*, pl. 82; Van Gelder and Borms, *op. cit.*; Benesch, *Northern Renaissance*, p. 100; *Tolnay II*, No. 57; C. G. Stridbeck, *Bruegels Fidesdarstellung*, *Konsthistorisk Tidskrift*, Stockholm, 1954, p. 1.

143 : Plate 140

CHARITAS. Rotterdam, Boymans-van Beuningen Museum (Koenigs Collection).

Pen and almost violet tones of brown ink. Crease in the centre. Somewhat faded in left foreground; damage in the upper left corner. 224×293 mm. Signed and dated at lower left corner, BRVEGEL *1559*. Watermark, an Imperial eagle. Preliminary drawing in reverse for the engraving, probably by Philippe Galle (Bastelaer, *Estampes*, No. 134). The word CHARITAS, and the inscription below it are in lighter ink and in another hand: *Speres tibi accidere quod alteri accidit, ita demum excitaberis ad opem ferendam si sumpseris eius animum qui opem tunc in malis constitutus implorat.*

Tolnay sees in this drawing a representation of the perverted world, but in this he is wrong. Among the models for this representation of Charitas are the two wings of an altar-piece by Barend van Orley (fig. 26). The basic scheme also recurs in a picture of the same subject by Martin van Heemskerk, which was also published a little later by Hieronymus Cock.

Lit.: *Michel*, p. 99; Van Gelder and Borms, *op. cit.*, pp. 10–11, pl. XI; Van Gils, *op. cit.*, III, pp, 12, and 35–41, fig. 7; *Vanbeselaere*, p. 43, fig. 15; *Ebbinge Wubben*, No. 50; Ludwig Münz, *Blick in die Welt*, London 1946/1947, No. 1, pp. 38–39; *Tolnay II*, No. 58.

144 : Plate 141

PRUDENTIA. Brussels, Musées Royaux des Beaux-Arts (Collection de Grez).

Pen and brown ink. 224×299 mm. Signed and dated at lower left corner, BRVEGHEL *1559*. Preliminary drawing, in reverse, for the engraving, probably by Philippe Galle, in Bastelaer, *Estampes*, No. 136. Inscribed below the central figure, PRUDENCIA, and along the lower margin, in another hand, *Si prudens esse cupis, in futurum prospectum ostende, et quae possunt contingere animo tuo cuncta propone.*

Except for a small damage near the left edge and the crease, this sheet is well preserved and shows a rich scale of tones ranging from light brown to dark-brown-violet in the shadows.

Lit.: Bastelaer, *Suite des dessins des Maîtres tirés de la Collection de Grez*, published by la Société des Bibliophiles et de Iconophiles de Belgique, Brussels, 1913; *Michel*, p. 99; L. van Puyvelde and E. Goldschmidt, *Dessins des Maîtres de la Collection des Musées Royaux des Beaux-Arts de Belgique*, Basle 1937, No. 2; Van Gelder and Borms, *op. cit.*, pp. 29 ff.; *Vanbeselaere*, p. 43; *Ebbinge Wubben*, No. 52; *Tolnay II*, No. 59.

145 : Plate 142

SPES. Berlin, Kupferstichkabinett.

Pen and greyish-brown ink. 224×295 mm. Signed and dated at lower right corner, BRVEGEL *1559*. Preliminary drawing, in reverse, for the engraving, probably by Philippe Galle, in Bastelaer, *Estampes*, No. 133. Inscribed below the central figure, SPES, and along the lower margin, in another hand, *Iucundissima est spei persvasio, et vite imprimis necessaria inter tot aerumnas peneq intolerabilis.*

Lit.: *Bastelaer*, No. 94; *Friedländer*, p. 68; *Michel*, pl. 83; Van Gelder and Borms, *op. cit.*; Bock-Rosenberg, *Berlin Catalogue*, No. 715; *Tolnay II*, No. 60.

146 : Plate 143

JUSTITIA. Brussels, Bibliothèque Royale, Cabinet des Estampes.

Pen and brownish ink. 223×295 mm. Signed and dated at lower left corner, *1559 BRVEGEL*. Formerly in the

W. Koller Collection, Vienna, and the Lanna Collection, Prague. Preliminary drawing, in reverse, for the engraving in Bastelaer, *Estampes*, No. 135. Inscribed below the central figure, JUSTICIA, and along the lower margin, in another hand, *Scopus legis est, aut ut eum quem punit emendet, aut poena eius ceteros meliores reddet aut sublatis malis ceteri securiores vivant.*

Parts of the drawing are largely derived from the woodcuts after Weiditz in Petrarch's *Trostspiegel*. In relation to Bruegel's work as a whole it is important to note that already in 1559 an execution scene is included in the far distance, as it is again later in *The Carrying of the Cross* of 1564.

Lit.: *Friedländer*, p. 67; Bastelaer, *Les dessins de P. Brueghel l'Ancien au Cabinet des Estampes de la Bibliothèque Royale de Belgique*, Société des Bibliophiles et des Iconophiles de Belgique, Brussels, 1924; *Michel*, pp. 99–100, pl. 84; Van Gelder and Borms, *op. cit.*, pp. 30–32, pl. XIII; Van Gils, *op. cit.*, III, pp. 55–66, pl. II; *Vanbeselaere*, p. 43, pl. 14; *Ebbinge Wubben*, No. 51; *Tolnay II*, No. 61.

147 : Plate 144

FORTITUDO. Rotterdam, Boymans-van Beuningen Museum (Koenigs Collection).

Pen and brownish-violet ink; dark stains at lower left corner. 224×293 mm. Signed at lower left corner, BRVEGEL, and dated at lower right corner, *1560*. Watermark, a double-headed eagle. Inscribed below the central figure FORTYTUDO. Preliminary drawing, in reverse for the engraving, Bastelaer, *Estampes*, No. 137.

Lit.: Benesch, *Old Master Drawings*, II, 1927 (June), pp. 2 f.; Van Gelder and Borms, *op. cit.*; *Tolnay II*, No. 62.

148 : Plate 145

TEMPERANTIA. Rotterdam, Boymans-van Beuningen Museum.

Pen and greyish-brown ink. 220×295 mm. Signed at lower left corner, BRVEGEL, and dated at lower right, *1560*. Watermark, an Imperial eagle. Inscribed, in mirror writing, at the bottom of the robe of the central figure, TEMPERANCIA, and along the lower margin, in another hand, *Videndum ut nec voluptati dediti prodigi et luxuriosi appareamus, nec avara tenacitati sordidi aut obscuri existamus.* Preliminary drawing, in reverse, for the engraving, Bastelaer, *Estampes*, No. 138.

Lit.: *Bastelaer*, No. 95; Van Gelder and Borms, *op. cit.*; *Tolnay II*, No. 63.

149 : Plate 146

CHRIST IN LIMBO. Vienna, Albertina.

Pen and blackish-brown ink. 224×292 mm. Signed at lower left corner, BRVEGEL. The date below this (*1561*) is on the same line as the inscription; in another hand, along the lower margin, *Tollite o porte capita vestra attolimine fores sempiterne et ingredietur Rex ille gloriosus.* Preliminary drawing,

in reverse, for the engraving by Pieter van der Heyden, Bastelaer, *Estampes*, No. 115.

Lit.: *Bastelaer*, No. 87; *Romdahl*, p. 111; Benesch, *Albertina Catalogue*, No. 79; Benesch, *Northern Renaissance*, p. 91; *Tolnay II*, No. 64.

The drawing *The Blind Men* (our No. 46) is listed among the landscapes of 1562.

150 : Plate 147

THE FALL OF THE MAGICIAN. Amsterdam, Rijksmuseum, Prentenkabinett.

Pen and darker and lighter brown ink. 222×292 mm. Signed and dated at lower left corner, BRVEGEL MDXLIIII (an error by Bruegel, it should read MDLXIIII). Watermark, an Imperial eagle. Preliminary drawing, in reverse, for the engraving, Bastelaer, *Estampes*, No. 118. Some signs of tracing.

The figure of the saint should be compared with the large *naer het leven* study *The Pilgrim* (our No. 102).

Lit.: *Bastelaer*, No. 88; E. W. Moes, *Handzeichnungen alter Meister im königlichen Kupferstichkabinett zu Amsterdam*, I, p. 21 (fascimile reproduction); *Michel*, p. 102 ('apocryphal'); *Tolnay II*, No. 66.

151 : Plate 148

SPRING. Vienna, Albertina. (Formerly in the Max Strauss Collection, Vienna; later in the Gottfried Eisler Collection, Vienna.)

Pen and lighter and darker brown ink. 223×289 mm. Signed and dated at lower right corner, MDLXV BRVEGEL. Preliminary drawing in reverse for Pieter van der Heyden's engraving, Bastelaer, *Estampes*, No. 200. Inscribed along the lower margin, *De lenten, Mert, April, Meij.*

This drawing is the first in a series of seasons, which was completed (*Autumn* and *Winter*) after Bruegel's death by Hans Bol, probably after sketches by Bruegel himself.

Lit.: *Bastelaer*, mentioned on p. 261, and *Estampes*, p. 62; Benesch, *Albertina Catalogue*, No. 83; *Michel*, p. 101; Benesch, *Northern Renaissance*, p. 102; F. Novotny, *Die Monatsbilder P. Bruegels d. Ae.*, Vienna, 1948, pl. 2; *Ebbinge Wubben*, No. 53; *Tolnay II*, No. 67.

152 : Plate 149

SUMMER. Hamburg, Kunsthalle.

Pen and darker and lighter brown ink; the paper turned yellowish-brown with age. 220×285 mm. Cut at left; and damaged at lower left and upper right corners. Dated below, in the centre, MDLXVIII, and signed at lower left corner (first letter cut away),—RVEGEL. Preliminary drawing, in reverse for the engraving, Bastelaer, *Estampes*, No. 202.

Lit.: *Bastelaer*, mentioned pp. 389–90; *Zeichnungen alter Meister in der Kunsthalle zu Hamburg, Niederländer*, N.F. 1926, Prestelgesellschaft, No. 8; *Michel*, p. 101, pl. 87; Friedländer,

Alt Niederländische Malerei, XIV, 1937, p. 38; Vanbeselaere, *P. Bruegel en het Nederlandsche manierisme*, 1944, p. 88, pl. 55; F. Novotny, *Die Monatsbilder P. Bruegels d. Ae.* Vienna, 1948, pl. 3; *Ebbinge Wubben*, No. 54; *Tolnay II*, No. 68.

153 : Plate 150

THE MARRIAGE OF MOPSUS AND NISA. New York, Metropolitan Museum (formerly Figdor Collection, Vienna).

Pen and brown ink. 266×416 mm. On wood. About or after 1566.

The drawing was executed on the wood block for subsequent cutting, which has already been begun in parts. This woodcut was probably designed to be the pair to the *Masquerade of Ourson and Valentine* (Bastelaer, *Estampes*, No. 215), which is signed on the right, BRVEGEL *1566*. Like the latter woodcut the present one includes an isolated group from *The Fight between Carnival and Lent*. Clearly no further work was done on this woodcut at the time of Bruegel's death, because an engraving by Pieter van der Heyden (Bastelaer, *Estampes*, No. 216), which shows the same group in reverse, was published by Cock in 1570, after Bruegel's death.

Lit.: Bastelaer, *Estampes*, No. 217; *Studies of the Metropolitan Museum*, New York, Vol. II.

154 : Plate 151

THE BEE-KEEPERS. Berlin, Kupferstichkabinett (formerly von Nagler Collection).

Pen and darker and lighter brown ink, on reddish-white paper. 203×309 mm. Signed and dated at lower right corner, BRVEGEL MDLXV. . . . The drawing has obviously been cut on the right, since the date ends with a V. The inscription at the lower left corner reads, *dye den nest weet dye weeten dyen Roft dy heeten*. About 1568.

This sheet is one of Bruegel's last drawings and was obviously intended for engraving. The most detailed explanation of this drawing, which has also been interpreted by Jedlicka, was published by Boström in 1949.

Lit.: *Bastelaer*, No. 100; *Friedländer*, p. 72; *Michel*, pl. 86; Bock-Rosenberg, *Berlin Catalogue*, No. 713; Gotthard Jedlicka, *Pieter Bruegel*, Zürich, 1938; Kjell Boström, *Das Sprichwort vom Vogelnest*, *Konsthistorisk Tidskrift*, Stockholm 1949, pp. 77 ff.; *Tolnay II*, No. 69.

DOUBTFUL LANDSCAPE DRAWINGS
ATTRIBUTED TO
PIETER BRUEGEL THE ELDER

A1 : Plate 153

SMALL SKETCH OF AN ITALIAN MONASTERY. (*Recto* of No. A2.)

Pen and light bistre, slightly tinted. 162×113 mm. Signature at lower left corner added later, *Peter Bragol*.

This drawing, together with that on the *verso*, was attributed to Bruegel by P. Wescher (*Pantheon*, IV, 1931, p. 182), and Benesch, in the Gilhofer & Ranschburg auction catalogue, Lucerne, 28.6.1934, lot 59, agrees with this attribution. Since we have no other rapid landscape sketches of this kind by Bruegel, this attribution ought at any rate to be taken into consideration, as in its line the drawing is related to our No. 2. Tolnay rejects both the *recto* and the *verso* of this sheet from the authentic works.

Lit.: P. Wescher, *Pantheon*, IV, April 1931, No. 4, *Bericht Beilage* XXV, repr. p. 182; Otto Benesch, *op. cit.*; *Tolnay II*, No. A13.

A2 : Plate 154

WOODED LANDSCAPE, WITH A CASTLE ON THE RIGHT. (*Verso* of No. A1.)

Silverpoint. 162×113 mm.

A3 : Plate 155

RIVER LANDSCAPE.

Etching. 211×325 mm.

This etching of a river landscape, of which only the one copy in Amsterdam has been preserved, shows, in reverse, a motif very similar to our No. 5, and in many respects it corresponds with Bruegel's style of drawing of the early 1550's.

Lit.: *Hollstein*, III, p. 255, No. 2a.

A4 : Plate 156

Anonymus Fabriczy. VIEW OF VIENNE. (*Recto* of No. A5.) Berlin, Kupferstichkabinett.

236×415 mm.

This sheet was copied by Braun Hogeberg for his etching, *Theatrum mundi*. Friedländer, 1921, and Bock-Rosenberg (*Berlin Catalogue*, No. 2233) considered both the *recto* and the *verso* of this sheet to be authentic drawings, which

Bruegel executed in France on his journey to Italy. Already in his 1925 edition Tolnay rejected this drawing and rightly attributed it to the Master of the Stuttgart Cabinet, Anonymus Fabriczy. Musper agrees with this attribution.

Lit.: *Friedländer*, 1921, pp. 39 f.; *Tolnay*, 1925 and 1935, p. 60, note 5; Th. Musper, *Der Anonymus Fabriczy*, in *J.d.pr.K.*, LVII, 1936, pp. 238 f.; Bock-Rosenberg, *Berlin Catalogue*, No. 2233; *Tolnay II*, No. A1.

A5 : Plate 157

Anonymus Fabriczy. VIEW OF A HILLY LANDSCAPE. (*Verso* of No. A4.) Berlin, Kupferstichkabinett.

236×415 mm.

A6 : Plate 158

Anonymus Fabriczy? VIEW OF FONDI. Private Collection in America.

Pen and brown ink.

In the opinion of Gustav Glück and W. Valentiner this drawing is by Pieter Bruegel the Elder, and Grossmann cites it as proof of Bruegel's journey to Italy. The style of the drawing, however, reveals a close relationship to that of Anonymus Fabriczy. It also seems to me that the handwriting on the *View of Vienne* (No. A4) is very closely related to that on this sheet.

Lit.: Gustav Glück, *Das grosse Bruegel-Werk*, Vienna, 1951, p. 7; F. Grossmann, *The Paintings of Bruegel*, London, 1955, p. 15.

A7 : Plate 159

Anonymus Fabriczy? MOUNTAIN RANGE. The Hague, Bredius Museum.

Pen and lighter and darker brown ink. 284×423 mm.

In his first edition Tolnay included this drawing, with certain doubts, among the authentic works, but in the second edition he rightly rejects it. He thinks that it is slightly later. Regteren Altena attributes it to J. de Gheyn, but it seems to me that with the thin lines of the contours of the mountains it is more closely related to drawings by Anonymus Fabriczy.

Lit.: *Tolnay II*, No. A10.

A8 : Plate 160

Jacques Savery. Landscape with a Castle on Rocks. Princeton, New Jersey, private collection.

Pen and yellowish ink, on white paper. 158×220 mm. Signed at lower left, *J. Savery*.

Placed by Tolnay, who dates it about 1558–59, at the beginning of the series of the small landscapes, this drawing, as a comparison with his etchings, which reveal the same rounded strokes, shows, is by Jacques Savery, whose signature is actually on the drawing. It must, therefore, have been executed later than 1559. A further drawing in the same style, now in Antwerp (our No. A10), was published by Delen as an Antwerp landscape of the second half of the sixteenth century.

Lit.: *Tolnay II*, No. 24.

A9 : Not reproduced

Jacques Savery. Landscape.

Etching.

This etching very clearly shows the same use of rounded strokes as in No. A8 above.

A10 : Plate 161

Jacques Savery. River Landscape with distant View. Antwerp, Musée Plantin-Moretus.

Pen and bistre. 275×370 mm.

This drawing, published by Delen as the work of one of the Antwerp landscape artists of the second half of the sixteenth century, is so closely related in its style to the two preceding drawings that it may well be considered as the work of Jacques Savery.

Lit.: J. J. Delen, *Catalogue des dessins anciens*, Brussels 1938, No. 3.

A11 : Plate 162

Jacques Savery? Ruined Tower. Paris, F. Lugt Collection.

Pen and light and darker brown ink. 156×211 mm. Signed and dated, JAQVES SAVERY F 1603.

This drawing shows the consistent way in which Savery used the style of Bruegel's small landscapes. Two drawings at Chatsworth, which I recognized as works by Jacques Savery, are related in their style to the present drawing.

A12 : Plate 163

Jacques Savery? Landscape with Church and Tower in the Distance. Rotterdam, Boymans-van Beuningen Museum. (Inv. No. 36.)

103×172 mm.

This sheet is reproduced as an example of a group of drawings which Friedländer, on the basis of a drawing in a private collection in America, attributed to Pieter Bruegel the Elder. The style of the draughtsmanship, however, which is particularly characteristic in the groups of trees, is rather to be related to that of Jacques Savery. Of this group, in addition to the present drawing and the one in America, which was published by Tietze, I also know one example now in the Louvre.

Lit.: Tietze, *European Master Drawings in the United States*, New York, 1947, No. 44.

A13 : Plate 164

Jacques Savery? Village Landscape. Berlin, Kupferstichkabinett.

Pen and lighter and darker brown ink. 155×217 mm. Signed with monogram, *IS*; and below this, in a later hand, *P. Bruegel*.

Friedländer attributed this drawing to Pieter Bruegel the Elder, but it was rightly rejected by Tolnay on account of its erratic draughtsmanship. The schematic imitation of the style of the small landscapes, as also the monogram *IS*, may be taken as evidence that this drawing could be by Jacques Savery.

Lit.: *Friedländer*, p. 128, fig. 69; Bock-Rosenberg, *Berlin Catalogue*, No. 4468.

A14 : Plate 166

Jacques Savery? Village Landscape with View of a Church. Amsterdam, Rijksmuseum, Prentenkabinett.

Pen and lighter and darker brown ink. 150×296 mm. Inscribed at lower left corner, in a different hand, *Bruegel*.

This landscape, mentioned by Tolnay under addenda 4 as apocryphal, and attributed by him to Roeland Savery, is so closely related in its draughtsmanship to the preceding drawing that it might well also be by Jacques Savery.

Lit.: *Tolnay II*, addenda No. 4.

A15 : Plate 165

Jacques Savery? Landscape with a Herd of Cattle and a Man with a Child and a Dog. Amsterdam, Rijksmuseum, Prentenkabinett.

Pen and lighter and darker brown ink. 148×387 mm.

Tolnay attributes this drawing to the Master of the Small Landscapes, but in its line it seems to me to be so close to the preceding drawing, that one is justified in thinking of the same artist, namely Jacques Savery.

Lit.: *Tolnay II*, addenda No. 5.

A16 : Plate 167

Roeland Savery? Landscape with the Martinswand near Innsbruck. Berlin, Kupferstichkabinett.

Pen and light brown ink, on white paper. 200×392 mm.

This drawing, the authenticity of which is supported by

Bastelaer, Pfister, Friedländer, the Berlin Catalogue, Benesch and Grossmann, appears to me, in the overall character of its line, not to be the work of Pieter Bruegel the Elder. In this I share Tolnay's opinion. Whether in this spiritless work we have a drawing by Roeland Savery – the line is closely related to that in our No. A19, which might also be by Roeland Savery – is not quite clear to me, although the way in which the figures are built up with fragmentary curves is very reminiscent of Roeland Savery's etching. Tolnay's identification of the scene as the Martinswand near Innsbruck is not altogether convincing. The identification is based on a drawing by G. Hoefnagel in the Kunsthistorisches Museum at Vienna, but in my opinion the resemblance is not sufficient to justify the opinion that our drawing shows the same place.

Lit.: *Bastelaer*, No. 19; *Friedländer*, p. 20; Bock-Rosenberg, *Berlin Catalogue*, No. 718; Benesch, *Kunstchronik*, 1953, p. 79; *Tolnay II*, No. A4; Grossmann, *Bulletin Boymans Museum*, 1954, Deel V, No. 2.

A17 : Plate 168

Georg Hoefnagel. THE MARTINSWAND NEAR ZIRL. Vienna, Kunsthistorisches Museum, Sammlung für Plastik und Kunstgewerbe.

Pen and lighter and darker brown ink. 200×455 mm.

This drawing is reproduced here for purposes of comparison with the *Martinswand* attributed to Bruegel (our No. A16).

A18 : Plate 169

Roeland Savery? SMALL CIRCULAR SHEET WITH LANDSCAPE. Leiden, Prentenkabinett.

Pen and brown ink in several tones, on white paper. Diameter, 105 mm.

Jan van Gelder and J. Q. van Regteren Altena consider this drawing to be the work of Bruegel, but I share Tolnay's doubts as to the authenticity of this sheet cut to form a circle, which, as can be seen from the edge, was obviously never any larger. In its style of drawing it is closest to Roeland Savery.

Lit.: *Tolnay II*, No. A14.

A19 : Plate 170

Roeland Savery? SMALL LANDSCAPE WITH A BROOK. Paris, F. Lugt Collection (Inv. No. 2391.)

Pen and lighter and darker brown ink. 142×193 mm. Signed at lower right corner, in black chalk, *R.S.*

This drawing, attributed by Friedländer to Bruegel, is only a free imitation of his style, and might well be by Roeland Savery, as the signature suggests and as Lugt supposed.

A20 : Plate 171

Roeland Savery. THE DREDGER. Chatsworth, Devonshire Collection.

Pen and yellowish ink. 190×328 mm.

In his 1925 edition Tolnay considered this drawing, first published as by Bruegel in the Vasari Society, Part VII, 1911–12, No. 18, to be authentic, but in 1935 he abandoned this attribution, and, on the basis of a comparison with a drawing in the Oppé Collection, London, he assigned it to Roeland Savery. A. E. Popham and E. Michel agree with him in this.

Lit.: Vasari Society, *loc. cit.*; Tolnay, *Die Zeichnungen Pieter Bruegels*, Munich 1925, No. 49; *Michel*, No. 102; Tolnay, *Pierre Bruegel l'Ancien*, Brussels 1935, Supplement, p. 103; A. E. Popham, *Catalogue of Drawings by Dutch and Flemish Artists in the British Museum*, Vol. V.; *Tolnay II*, No. A15.

A21 : Plate 172

Imitator of Bruegel (Jan Brueghel the Elder?). VIEW OF A HILLSIDE WITH A VILLAGE ON THE RIGHT. Paris, Louvre (Inv. No. 19732).

Pen and lighter and darker brown ink. Signed on a rock below on the right, *P.B.*

In the whole style of its draughtsmanship this drawing, which was etched by Cajus in the eighteenth century (Bastelaer, *Estampes*, No. 95), is very close to Bruegel, but the more stylized treatment of the foliage of the trees, especially in the shadows, and the softer strokes, suggest that it is not by him. In their rhythm the strokes used in the trees on the hillside are especially closely related to those in the foreground details on the right of the following drawing. There is much in this drawing to support the theory that this is a copy after a lost work by Pieter Bruegel the Elder.

A22 : Plate 173

Jan Brueghel the Elder? MOUNTAIN LANDSCAPE. Brunswick, Landesmuseum.

Pen and lighter and darker brown ink. 203×294 mm.

Flechsig published this drawing as an authentic early work by Bruegel, while Tolnay rightly rejects it. In my opinion it is by Jan Brueghel the Elder, as a comparison with the style of drawing of the trees in the sheet of the *Road to Emmaus* at Rotterdam (No. A23 below) proves.

Lit.: Flechsig, *Zeichnungen Alter Meister im Landesmuseum zu Braunschweig*, Prestelgesellschaft, No. 53; *Tolnay II*, No. A3.

A23 : Plate 174

Jan Brueghel the Elder. LANDSCAPE WITH THE ROAD TO EMMAUS. Rotterdam, Boymans-van Beuningen Museum (Inv. No. 86).

Pen and lighter and darker brown ink, cut to an oval. 244×373 mm.

The nervous style of drawing in the figures is so close to that found in Jan Brueghel the Elder's Italian landscape drawings, that the attribution of this sheet to him seems justified. In Rotterdam the drawing is described as a work by Pieter Bruegel the Elder.

A24 : Plate 175

Jan Brueghel the Elder? THE RIPA GRANDE IN ROME. Chatsworth, Devonshire Collection.

Pen and brown ink in several tones. The dark foreground stands out from the light middle distance and the very light background on the right. 207×285 mm. Inscribed above in the centre, *a rypa*.

Egger was the first to introduce this drawing into the literature as the work of Pieter Bruegel, though it is significant that he mentions other drawings of 1559 and 1560 as stylistically related to it. Even today it is still considered to be an authentic work by Pieter Bruegel, but I am convinced that the original attribution to Jan Brueghel the Elder is the correct one. Certain inter-related flourishes in the drawing, and also the schematic division between foreground, middle distance and background, support this assumption. The drawing can certainly not be accepted as documentary evidence of Pieter Bruegel's having worked in Rome in 1553. The most detailed recent discussion of representations of the Ripa Grande by artists of the sixteenth and seventeenth centuries is that of Roger d'Hulst. For the style of drawing of the figures, with the outlines stronger on the one side and lighter on the other, see No. A27 among the Jan Brueghel drawings reproduced here.

Lit.: Egger, *Römische Veduten*, Leipzig, 1911, Vol. I, pl. 70; *Friedländer*, p. 41, fig. 23; *Vasari Society*, 2nd Series, Part VI, 1925, pl. 11; *Michel*, p. 91, pl. 64; *Ebbinge Wubben*, No. 44; Roger d'Hulst, *De 'Ripa Grande' te Rome, Bulletin des Musées Royaux des Beaux-Arts*, No. 3, Brussels, September, 1952, pp. 103 ff.; F. Grossmann, *op. cit.*, No. 3, p. 84; *Tolnay II*, No. 4.

A25 : Plate 176

Jan Brueghel the Elder. TRIUMPHAL ARCH. Chatsworth, Devonshire Collection.

Pen and lighter and darker brown ink. Signed on the arch, BRUEGHEL 1594.

This drawing is reproduced here because in the style of drawing, especially of parts of the right and left background, it is almost identical with the landscape in the right background of the *a rypa* drawing. This also applies to the way in which, on the left, whole portions of the landscape and undergrowth are summarized in one flourish of the pen.

A26 : Plate 177

Jan Brueghel the Elder. BASRODE. Berlin, Kupferstichkabinett.

Pen and lighter and darker brown ink. 250×421 mm. The signature BRUEGEL on the right is not in the artist's hand. This drawing was attributed by Friedländer to Pieter

Bruegel the Elder, but it was rightly rejected by Tolnay. The handwriting is very similar to that on No. A24. In Berlin there is another slightly weaker drawing of Basrode.

Lit.: *Friedländer*, p. 150; Bock-Rosenberg, *Berlin Catalogue*, No. 5763.

A27 : Plate 178

Jan Brueghel the Elder. BASRODE. London, British Museum, Print Room.

Pen and lighter and darker brown ink. 200×319 mm.

This drawing was originally in the Fenwick Collection and was first published by A. E. Popham in the Catalogue of that collection. In view of its whole style of drawing, including that of the figures, it must be by Jan Brueghel the Elder.

Lit.: A. E. Popham, *Fenwick Collection Catalogue*, 1935.

A28 : Plate 179

Jan Brueghel the Elder? FOREST LANDSCAPE WITH BEARS. London, British Museum, Print Room.

Pen and brown ink. 336×232 mm.

F. Lugt, speaking of this and another drawing with bears in the same collection, rightly refers to Muziano as the inspirer of such works, but I think that Lugt goes too far when he claims that this is an authentic work by Pieter Bruegel the Elder. The style of drawing of some of the foliage and the characteristic flourishes in some parts, are too reminiscent of Jan Brueghel the Elder's drawings, such as those in Rotterdam and Milan. Whether this and the following drawing were based on models by Jan Brueghel's father, is a problem which I have been unable to solve.

Lit.: F. Lugt, *Festschrift für M. Friedländer, op. cit.*; Benesch, *Kunstchronik*, 1953, pp. 76 f.; A. M. Hind, *Drawings by Dutch and Flemish Artists in the British Museum*, Vol. II, p. 92, No. 1.

A29 : Plate 180

Jan Brueghel the Elder. THE ANGLER. Brussels, Musées Royaux.

Pen and brown ink in several tones. Signed in a later hand, *Bruegel 1556*.

This drawing of an angler, which is by the same hand as the preceding drawing, bears the date *1556* next to a late signature, and this can be taken as an indication that drawings of this type by Pieter Bruegel the Elder may have existed.

Lit.: F. Lugt, *Festschrift für M. Friedländer, op. cit.*

A30 : Plate 182

Jan Brueghel the Elder. ALPINE LANDSCAPE WITH PINE FOREST. Rotterdam, Boymans-van Beuningen Museum (Koenigs Collection).

Pen and brown ink, on reddish-white paper. 216×300 mm.

Tolnay rightly rejects this drawing. To me it seems to be by the same hand as the landscape drawing with the *Road to Emmaus* in Rotterdam (our No. A23), which is probably by Jan Brueghel the Elder. There is a second, partly coloured, copy of this landscape in Munich, inscribed BRVEGHEL *1603* [our No. A31]. A drawing in the Lugt Collection also repeats major portions of this landscape in a summary way. The painting in Vienna of 1562 with the suicide of Saul has a pine forest in the right background, which, in its main features, coincides with this drawing. Tolnay, however, only mentions the fact that the rock in the middle of the drawing is repeated in a similar form in the painting.

Lit.: *Tolnay II*, No. A9.

A31 : Plate 185

Jan Brueghel the Elder. ALPINE LANDSCAPE WITH PINE FOREST. Munich, Staatliche Graphische Sammlungen.

Pen and ink and water-colours. 219×303 mm. Signed on the rock in the centre, BRVEGHEL *1603*.

This drawing repeats with slight variations the landscape of our No. A30.

A32 : Plate 181

Jan Brueghel the Elder? ALPINE LANDSCAPE WITH FOREST. Paris, F. Lugt Collection.

Pen and lighter and darker brown ink. 185×244 mm.

This very hasty drawing is a further variation of the two preceding landscapes. It is reproduced here because in its style of drawing it is very reminiscent of our Nos. A21 and A22.

A33 : Plate 183

Jan Brueghel the Elder? HUT WITH FENCE. (*Recto* of No. A34.) Munich, Staatliche Graphische Sammlungen.

Pen and brown ink. 95×139 mm.

Already in the first edition of his book Tolnay relegated this drawing, which was attributed to Pieter Bruegel the Elder by Bastelaer and Romdahl, to the apocryphal drawings. The present drawing, and even more so that on the *verso* of the sheet, remind me rather of the meticulous strokes of some of the earlier work of Jan Brueghel the Elder, although in some respects they are related to the so-called small landscapes by Cock.

Lit.: *Bastelaer*, No. 10; *Romdahl, op. cit.*; *Tolnay I*, 1925, p.73.

A34 : Plate 184

Jan Brueghel the Elder? BARN. (*Verso* of No. A33.) Munich, Staatliche Graphische Sammlungen.

Pen and brown ink. 95×139 mm.

The draughtsmanship of this *verso* seems to me particularly close to that of Jan Brueghel the Elder.

Lit.: *Bastelaer*, No. 11.

A35 : Plate 186

Jan Brueghel the Elder. TOWN WITH BRIDGE. Basle, Baron R. von Hirsch Collection.

Pen and wash.

This drawing by Jan Brueghel the Elder is reproduced here to show that he was quite able to apply the correct wash to a drawing, so that there is no reason to think of Claude Lorrain as the author of the *Vista of Reggio* (our No. 26), despite the fact that the latter's name appears twice on the back of it.

Lit.: G. Swarzenski and E. Schilling, *op. cit.*, No. 33.

A36 : Plate 187

Master of 1572? ROCKY ISLAND. Milan, Ambrosiana.

This drawing was first published by Benesch as by Jan van Scorel. Tolnay considers the possibility that it might be a very early drawing by Pieter Bruegel the Elder, but the style of the drawing supports the attribution to a master of the older generation, related to Matthys Cock, who must, however, in my opinion, have lived longer than this artist, since the style of the drawing of the present sheet is very close to that of an artist, one drawing by whom, in the Louvre, is dated 1572.

Lit.: Benesch, *Graphische Künste*, Vol. LV, 1932, *Mitteilungen des Vereins für vervielfältigende Kunst*, p. 7, fig. 5a; *Tolnay II*, No. A7.

COPIES

MOSTLY AFTER LOST DRAWINGS BY PIETER BRUEGEL THE ELDER, AND DRAWINGS BY PIETER BRUEGHEL THE YOUNGER

A37 : Plate 188

MAN POURING OUT WATER. Paris, Louvre (Inv. No. 19722).

Pen and brown ink. 143×95 mm.

This drawing, which Baldass attributed to Bosch, is very closely connected with Bruegel's work. The composition of this drawing is so closely related to the fifth roundel of the twelve Flemish proverbs in the Mayer van den Bergh Collection, Antwerp, that it might easily be a preliminary sketch for this. We know too little about Bruegel's quick pen sketches to be able to express a definite opinion, but it is certainly possible that the present drawing and the whole painting of the twelve Flemish proverbs are by Pieter Brueghel the Younger.

Lit.: L. von Baldass, *Hieronymus Bosch*, Vienna, 1943, p. 253; *Bastelaer*, No. 81.

A38 : Plate 189

THREE MEN IN CONVERSATION. Göttingen, Staats- und Universitätsbibliothek.

Pen, probably with brown ink. 82×98 mm. Colour indications.

According to the University Library in Göttingen, this drawing, which was first mentioned by Stechow and which I have not myself seen, measures 82×98 mm. It is probably a later copy. The figure of the alchemist on the left is very similar to that on our No. 109.

Lit.: *Tolnay II*, No. A32.

A39 : Plate 190

THREE PEASANTS. Ghent, Delacre Collection.

Pen. 196×250 mm.

In addition to the copy of a man seen from the back on the drawing in the Boymans-van Beuningen Museum, Rotterdam (our No. 116), this drawing has two further figures on the left, which are probably copies after a lost drawing by Pieter Bruegel. The style of the drawing, however, is closest to Pieter Brueghel the Younger.

Lit.: *Tolnay II*, No. A32.

A40 : Plate 191

A MASKED MAN. Berlin, Kupferstichkabinett.

Pen and brown ink. 251×94 mm. Inscribed below, *J. Callot 32*.

Friedländer considered this to be a drawing by Pieter Bruegel the Elder, but to me it seems more likely that it is a drawing by the younger Brueghel.

Lit.: *Friedländer*, p. 119, fig. 65; Bock-Rosenberg, *Berlin Catalogue*, No. 4637.

A41 : Plate 192

A MAN WALKING; BEHIND HIM A WOMAN WITH A CHILD IN HER ARMS. Ghent, Delacre Collection.

Pen.

This drawing by Pieter Brueghel the Younger may also be a copy after Pieter Bruegel the Elder. It must be connected with the group of drawings by Pieter Brueghel the Younger related to the *Wedding Procession*.

A42 : Plate 194

PEASANT WOMAN LEADING A DRUNKEN MAN HOME. Frankfurt am Main, Städelsches Kunstinstitut (Inv. No. 3774).

Pen. 177×132 mm.

This drawing of a peasant woman leading home a drunken man, mentioned by several authors as the work of Pieter Bruegel the Elder, is actually, like the following drawing, by Pieter Brueghel the Younger, and both drawings were used for the latter's painting in the Grisar Collection of Antwerp.

Lit.: *Bastelaer*, No. 43.

A43 : Plate 193

BRAWLING PEASANTS.

The brawling peasants in the background of the painting in the Grisar Collection at Antwerp are found in this drawing, which was sold at auction in Vienna as the work of Pieter Bruegel the Elder. It is, however, also by Pieter Brueghel the Younger.

Lit.: *Auction Catalogue No. 181*, Kunsthaus Kende, Vienna, May 1952, lot 438.

A44 : Plate 195

The painting in the Grisar Collection at Antwerp is reproduced here from Bastelaer, in order to show how Pieter Brueghel the Younger used such studies.

A45 : Plate 196

Jacques Savery. THE PAINTER AND THE CONNOISSEUR. (Copy after the original by Bruegel, No. 126.) Formerly in the collection of Dr. Eberhard Kornfeld, Berne.

Pen and brown ink. Sold Klipstein and Kornfeld, Bern, Auction 98, 16 June, 1960, lot 44, repr. pl. 24 – attributed to Bruegel. 314×222 mm.

A46 : Plate 198

THE PAINTER AND THE CONNOISSEUR. (Copy after the original by Bruegel, No. 126.) London, Vincent Korda Collection.

Pen and brown ink. 298×219 mm.

This copy was wrongly published by Tolnay as an original by Bruegel.

Lit.: Tolnay, *Les Arts Plastiques*, 1948, pp. 455 f.; *Ebbinge Wubben*, No. 43; *Tolnay II*, No. 119.

A47 : Plate 197

Georg Hoefnagel. THE PAINTER AND THE CONNOISSEUR. (Copy after the original by Bruegel, No. 126.) Vienna, Christian Nebehay.

272×216 mm.

'The identification of the artist is based on an old inscription on the back: *vom Hufnagel 1602*. This is probably a note by a Viennese owner, since the writer inscribed it on the sheet after Hoefnagel's death. The high quality of this copy reveals the hand of an excellent artist, so that, without knowing the original, one would be tempted to consider it as by Bruegel himself. It is not impossible that both Savery and Hoefnagel worked in Bol's studio at about the same time and drew from this model. This may have happened in Antwerp, where Bol was from 1572 to 1584 and Hoefnagel from 1570 to 1576'. (Quoted from Benesch, *Katalog der Frühjahrsausstellung der Albertina*, Vienna, 1956.)

A48 : Plate 199

THE PAINTER AND THE CONNOISSEUR. (Copy after the original by Bruegel, No. 126.) London, British Museum.

Pen and greyish-brown ink. 261×207 mm. Inscribed at lower left corner, *P. Breugel fecit*. Upper corners cut off.

This copy in the British Museum is the weakest in the series of copies after Pieter Bruegel's original.

Lit.: *Bastelaer*, p. 201, No. 104; Popham, *Catalogue of Dutch and Flemish Drawings in the British Museum*, Vol. 5, p. 145, No. 8.

A49 : Plate 200

Pieter Brueghel the Younger. DANCERS AT A VILLAGE WEDDING. Preliminary drawing for Hollar's etching, Passavant 597. London, British Museum.

Pen, brown ink and wash, over preliminary drawing in black chalk. 241×380 mm.

This drawing, placed by Popham under the copies after Bruegel (No. 12), is obviously by Pieter Brueghel the Younger. Parts of this copy are derived from various engravings after Bruegel, namely: the wedding group in the background of Bastelaer, *Estampes*, No. 210, as also the kissing couple in the centre and the dancing peasants in the foreground; the landscape in the right background from *The Bee-Keepers* (our No. 154). In addition there are the two following drawings by Pieter Brueghel the Younger (No's. A50 and A51), which probably also derive from his father.

Lit.: Popham, *Catalogue of Drawings by Dutch and Flemish Artists in the British Museum*, Vol. V, p. 146, No. 12.

A50 : Plate 201

Pieter Brueghel the Younger. GROUP OF MEN AND WOMEN. Budapest, National Gallery.

The preliminary drawing for the group on the right is preserved in Budapest, and is mentioned by Meder (No. 1135) as a copy after Pieter Bruegel the Elder.

Lit.: Schönbrunner-Meder, *Handzeichnungen alter Meister in der Albertina und anderen Sammlungen*, No. 1135.

A51 : Plate 202

Pieter Brueghel the Younger. SHEET OF STUDIES. Besançon, Musée des Beaux-Arts.

The group of three men on the right of Pieter Brueghel the Younger's *Peasant Wedding* is based on the three men in the centre of this drawing at Besançon. Both the figures to the left and right of this group in the drawing are very close in their manneristic verve to Pieter Bruegel the Elder's late drawings, and might be copies after a work by him.

A52 : Not Reproduced

Pieter Brueghel the Younger. KERMESS. Vienna, Albertina. Water-colour.

This water-colour, first mentioned by Hausenstein, is placed here because, like No. A49, it is a composition after drawings by the elder Bruegel, of which the following have been preserved: the team of horses in the centre is found in the drawing *Team of Horses* at the Albertina (our No. 105); a woman on the right appears in the engraving Bastelaer, *Estampes*, No. 59.

Lit.: W. Hausenstein, *Der Bauern-Bruegel*, Munich, 1910, fig. 45.

A53 : Not Reproduced

Pieter Brueghel the Younger. THE PAINTER AT HIS EASEL. Paris, Louvre.

Pen and yellowish-brown ink, on white paper.

This drawing, as has already been suggested by Tolnay, is by Pieter Brueghel the Younger. There is a copy of it in the Louvre (*Tolnay II*, No. A19b), bearing the inscription, *Bruegel. Nulla dies abeat quin linea ducta supersit*; a second copy is in the Musée Bonnat at Bayonne (*Tolnay II*, No. A19a).

Lit.: *Tolnay II*, No. A19, pl. LXXXIII.

A54 : Fig.17

Pieter Brueghel the Younger? A FOOL SITTING ON AN EGG AND DRINKING. British Museum, London.

Dated 1569.

Of the drawings connected with the twelve proverbs only the present one is reproduced in the present volume, because it is very possible that this re-drawing is derived from a drawing made by Pieter Bruegel the Elder in the last year of his life.

Lit.: *Bastelaer*, No. 102.

COMPOSITIONS BY BRUEGEL PRESERVED ONLY IN DRAWINGS, AND COPIES AFTER HIS COMPOSITIONS

[Dr. Münz had planned to publish most of the drawings preserved in the form of engravings in a separate volume devoted to Bruegel's engravings. In this volume he had also meant to include the drawings for the twelve proverbs, of which only one is reproduced here, No. A. 54.]

A55 : Plate 203

Copy after Pieter Bruegel. THE EPILEPTIC WOMEN OF MEULEBEECK. Vienna, Albertina (Inv. No. 7868).

Pen and brown ink, on white paper, heightened with white. 286×414 mm. Inscribed, *dit sin dije pelgerommen die op sint Jans dach buijten te meulebeec danssen moeten ende als sij over een brugge gedanst oft gesprongen hebben dan sin sij genesen vor een heel Jaer van sint Jans sieckte, bruegel 1564*. The drawing was engraved by H. Hondius (The Hague, 1642).

This drawing, which Romdahl, Rooses and Bastelaer held to be authentic, was recognized as a copy by Tolnay and Benesch. In its style it is so closely related to drawings by Pieter Brueghel the Younger, that it might well be his work. A copy in the Rijksmuseum, Amsterdam, is mentioned by Bastelaer.

Lit.: Romdahl, *op. cit.*, p. 136, pl. XXI; Rooses, *Onze Kunst*, I, p. 192; Bastelaer, *Estampes*, Nos. 222–4. Copy in the Rijksmuseum, Amsterdam, Bastelaer, *op. cit.*; p. 191; *Tolnay I*, 1925, p. 74; Benesch, *Albertina Catalogue*, No. 86.

A56 : Not reproduced

Copy after Pieter Bruegel the Elder, probably by Pieter Brueghel the Younger. THREE PILGRIMS. London, British Museum.

Pen, brown ink and blue wash. 204×264 mm. The signature *bruegel 1566* at lower right is not in Bruegel the Elder's own hand.

This drawing was first published by Campbell Dodgson in the *Vasari Society*, Vol. 8, No. 21. A copy is in Munich, and there is said to be a second copy in Stockholm. In its style the present drawing is very close to the drawing of the epileptic woman. There seems to be no objection to dating the original drawing by Pieter Bruegel the Elder to the year indicated in the inscription, 1566. I do not see the reason why the pilgrims should be blind, as Campbell Dodgson suggests in his title.

Lit.: *Vasari Society*, Vol. 8, No. 21.

A57 : Plate 204

A. van Dyck after Bruegel. STUDY FOR THE FEAST OF ST. MARTIN.

The three drawings on this sheet, which Burchard has hitherto attributed, together with a drawing of the Massacre of the Innocents, to Rubens himself, are, as he has since stated, by Van Dyck. The sheet shows a very rough sketch of brawling peasants, to the left of which, on an attached piece of paper, is a drunken peasant being taken home by two women, and beneath this a scene of beggars warming themselves before a fire at the Feast of St. Martin. The lower group reappears in Pieter Balten's painting of the Feast of St. Martin in Antwerp. Yet the style of the drawing is such a deliberate imitation of Bruegel's draughtsmanship, that one can state with some certainty that these sketches by Van Dyck were actually copied from drawings by Pieter Bruegel the Elder, and not from a painting.

A58 : Not reproduced

THE ASCENSION OF CHRIST. Rotterdam, Boymans-van Beuningen Museum (F. Koenigs Collection).

Pen, brown ink, and grey wash, over preliminary drawing in red chalk. 425×306 mm. Some damage in the light parts near the hearth on the left.

This very badly preserved sheet, first published by W. Cohen, agrees with the engraving Bastelaer, *Estampes*, No. 114, and is rightly considered not to be an authentic work by Bruegel. Grossmann's attempt to prove it authentic seems to me entirely mistaken. The weak inner drawing of the figures should have been sufficient to dissuade him from making such an assertion.

Lit.: W. Cohen, *Wallraf-Richartz Jahrbuch*, Vol. I, 1924, pp. 114 f.; *Tolnay II*, No. A21; F. Grossmann, *The Paintings of Bruegel*, London, 1955, p. 192, plates 30 and 31.

LIST OF ADDENDA

(by Luke Herrmann)

Drawings attributed to Pieter Bruegel the Elder, first published since Dr. Münz's death.

Appendix 1

ALPINE LANDSCAPE. London, British Museum.

Pen and brown ink. 171×543 mm. About 1555.

Lit.: Christopher White, *Pieter Bruegel the Elder: Two New Drawings, Burlington Magazine*, Vol. CI, 1959, p. 336, fig. 44.

App. 2

ALPINE LANDSCAPE. London, Count Antoine Seilern Collection.

Pen and ink. 247×432 mm. Inscribed and dated at lower left corner, *P. Brueghel 1547.*

Lit.: Sotheby's Sale, November 27, 1957, lot 37a (property of Mrs. G. M. W. Huggill), reproduced; F. Grossmann, *New Light on Bruegel, Burlington Magazine*, Vol. CI, 1959, p. 345.

App. 3

MOUNTAIN LANDSCAPE WITH FOUR TRAVELLERS. Northampton, Mass., Smith College Museum of Art.

Pen and light brown ink, on cream paper. 140×189 mm. Signed and dated at lower left corner, P. BRUEGEL *1560.*

Lit: *Great Master Drawings of Seven Centuries*, Exhibition at M. Knoedler and Company, New York, October–November 1959, No. 23 (catalogue note by Leonard Slatkes), pl. XXIII; Tolnay, *Remarques sur Quelques Dessins de Bruegel l'Ancien, Musées Royaux des Beaux-Arts Bulletin*, Brussels, 1960, 1–2, p. 17, fig. 10.

App. 4

LANDSCAPE WITH A VILLAGE CHURCH. London, Private Collection. (Not reproduced here.)

Pen and ink. 201×305 mm. Signed and dated, *1562.*

Lit.: Sotheby's Sale, June 26, 1957, lot 4; F. Grossmann, *loc. cit.*, p. 345.

App. 5

PEASANT CARRYING A JAR. (*Recto* of App. 6.) Lully-sur-Morges, N. Chaikin Collection.

Pen and ink over preliminary drawing in black chalk. 154×80 mm. Inscribed at lower margin, *Naer het leven.*

[The owner suggests that the figure represents an almsgiver.]

Lit.: Tolnay, *loc. cit.*, pp. 18–20, fig. 12.

App. 6

BACK VIEW OF A PEASANT IN A CLOAK. (*Verso* of App. 5.) Lully-sur-Morges, N. Chaikin Collection. (Not reproduced here.)

Black chalk. 154×80 mm.

Lit.: Tolnay, *loc. cit.*, pp. 19–20, fig. 13.

App. 7

PEASANT SEEN FROM THE BACK. (*Verso* of Cat. No. 88.) Vorden (Huize de Wiersse), Mme A. Gatacre-de Stuers Collection.
Black chalk. 161×100 mm.

Lit.: J. G. van Gelder, *Pieter Bruegel: 'Na(e)rt Het Leven', Musées Royaux des Beaux Arts Bulletin*, Brussels, 1960, 1–2, p. 32, fig. 2.

App. 8

THE CALUMNY OF APELLES. London, British Museum.

Pen and brown ink with brown wash. There are touches of oxidized white heightening, probably added later. 204×307 mm. Signed and dated at lower right corner, P. BRUEGEL M.D.LXV (partially reworked).

This sheet was discovered in a sale at Sotheby's (January 21, 1959, from lot 2).

Lit.: Christopher White, *loc. cit.*, pp. 336 f., fig. 45.

ADDENDA : ILLUSTRATIONS

App. 1. ALPINE LANDSCAPE. About 1555. London, British Museum

App. 2. ALPINE LANDSCAPE. Dated 1547. London, Count Antoine Seilern Collection

App. 3. Mountain Landscape with Four Travellers. Dated 1560. Northampton, Mass., Smith College Museum of Art

App. 7. Peasant Seen from the Back. (Verso of Cat. No. 88 above.) Vorden (Huize de Wiersse), Mme Gatacre-de Stuers

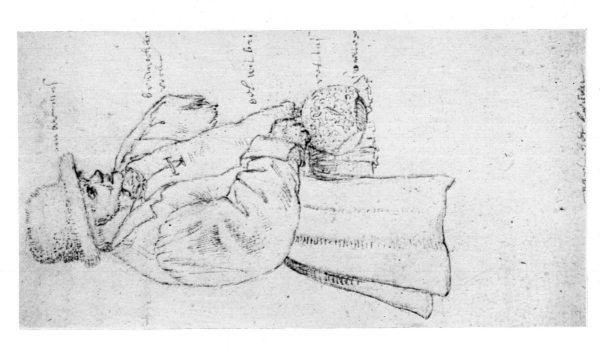

App. 5. Peasant Carrying a Jar
Lully-sur-Morges, N. Chaikin Collection

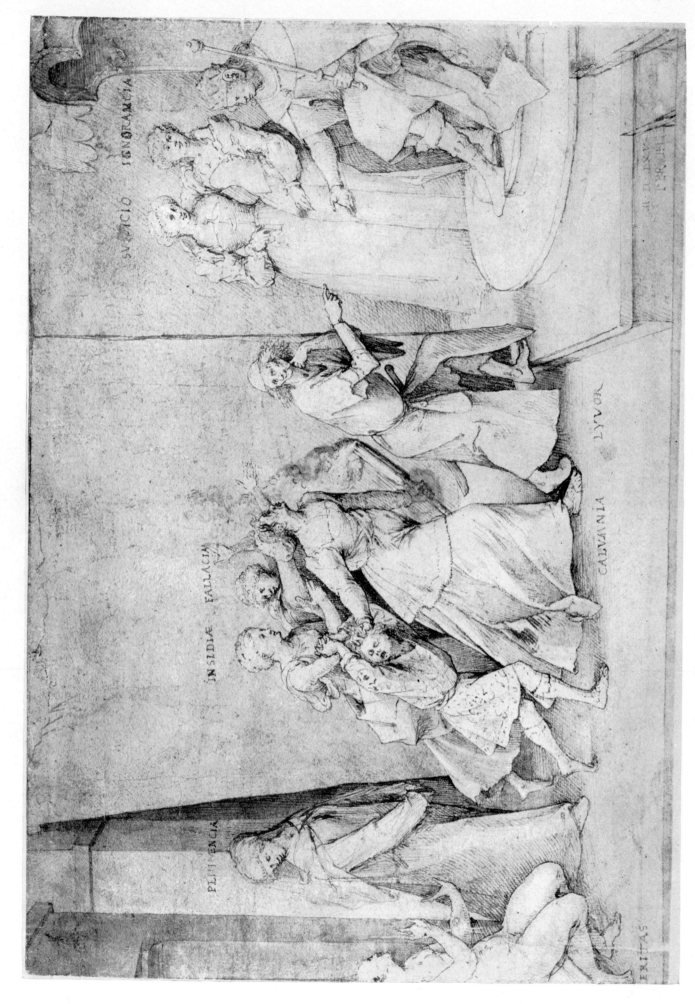

App. 8. THE CALUMNY OF APELLES. Dated 1565. London, British Museum

LIST OF COLLECTIONS

The numbers refer to the Catalogue.